James Baldwin's
Another Country:

BOOKMARKED

KIM MCLARIN

PUBLISHING

New York, NY

Ig Publishing
Box 2547
New York, NY 10163
www.igpub.com

ISBN: 978-1-63246-121-6

PRINTED IN THE UNITED STATES OF AMERICA

FIRST EDITION | FIRST PRINTING

For Ray.
For once in my life.

PART ONE

Why I Write

The crime of which you discover slowly you are guilty is not so much that you are aware, which is bad enough, but that other people see that you are and cannot bear to watch it, because it testifies to the fact that they are not. You're bearing witness helplessly to something which everybody knows and nobody wants to face.—James Baldwin

I USED TO SAY THERE were no baby pictures of me, the forgotten middle child. This was a statement that felt true even if what it implied—abundant photos of my mother's four other children—was not. There aren't many pictures in general, just a few group shots of us three oldest girls, followed by more frequent and casual snaps of the late-stage, exciting twins. The reasons for this paucity of photos—my mother's full hands, my parents' deteriorating marriage, the high price of film—are less revealing than the way my brain packaged the situation. I told myself a story of invisibility and outsiderness, portrait of the artist as an outcast, right from the start. Writers are full of themselves because that's the first thing we eat.

At least I can say I came by it honest. My mother, who has rarely met a person she was not afraid would mistreat her if given the chance, is an outsider of the first order. The only years she really felt like she belonged were her earliest ones, spent on her grandfather's Mississippi farm. For years my mother mentioned these days and for years it failed to occur to me what it meant for a Black man to own land in the Delta in 1940. Not until I read a story in *The Atlantic* about the theft of Black land did it occur to me to wonder.

Turns out my great grandfather was not alone. After the Civil War thousands of freedmen, driven by what W.E.B. DuBois called "land hunger" and encouraged by his Atlanta-compromising peer (and sometimes nemesis) Booker T. Washington, grabbed up every acre they could beg, buy, or barter from white landowners across the south. My mother remembers her grandfather's farm as a self-sufficient (and completely colored) paradise, blessed with fish-stocked ponds and pecan trees and enough freshly grown vegetables and egg-laying chickens to feed everyone. Paradise was disrupted when she was sent to live with her father and his schoolteacher wife. My mother missed the farm, but her new stepmother was kind and childless, which meant no half-siblings against which to compete. She taught my mother to read and write and value education. "The only thing they can't take away is what's in your head."

The rest of my mother's childhood was far less golden, but she remembered her stepmother's advice. At eighteen she got on a bus and headed east to knock on the door of Knoxville College, a small HBCU. They took her in, put her in a room with two other girls, and gave her a job in the cafeteria to pay her tuition. In the summers she was sent north to work for white people. That's where she met my father, a Navy seaman. She left college, a decision she would deeply regret. Five children later, she found herself divorced, back home in Memphis with five little mouths to feed and five little bodies to shelter and five little hearts to attend. It was a Herculean task, one she managed heroically. We never starved and we were never homeless. Our hearts, however, were on their own.

Are writers born? Are writers made?

In *On Becoming a Novelist*, the writer-teacher John Gardner suggests "what the writer probably needs most is an almost demonic compulsiveness. A psychological wound is helpful, if it can be kept in partial control, to keep the novelist driven. Some childhood accident ..."

Does anyone survive childhood without a psychic

wound? Certainly, my own bruises did not match Gardner's in intensity: he accidentally ran over and killed his brother while driving a tractor. One can only imagine the ensuing trauma. But so many things can wound a child. We, for example, were impoverished. Poverty is like water: it takes the form of its container. The poverty of my husband's family —white, Catholic, two-parent, and northern—was in some ways similar to (stitched-together meals, the dodging of creditors) and in some ways different from (crowded apartment versus crowded house, parents who had not gone to college versus a mother who had) our Black, Pentecostal, one-parent, southern existence. For a child, the hardships of our kind of poverty (cheap meals, heating water on the stove because the water heater is broken, taking the bus because the car needs fixing, rising at four in the morning for a newspaper route) are not harmful. It is the humiliation which wounds, especially when that humiliation becomes attached to some intrinsic part of oneself.

Growing up I knew nothing about Daniel Patrick Moynihan or his influential 1965 report *The Negro Family* but it was pretty clear to me that the reason we were poor was because we were Black. Sure, our father not living with us didn't help things, but my uncle lived with his family and they were still poor. So were the folks up the street and so was my maiden Aunt Pearl and so were a lot of other people, all of them Black. This was not true, as far as I knew, of any of the white kids with whom I went to school and it certainly wasn't true of any of the white folks on television. My husband, offhand, mentions identifying with the poverty of *The Waltons*. I look at him in surprise: "The Waltons were poor? Did you see the size of that house?"

Standing in long, hot lines outside a government office with my mother to get food stamps was not hard but was shameful. *Temporary layoffs!* Tearing food stamps as colorful as comics out of a book at the checkout line was not hard but was humiliating, as was being called to the front of the room every Monday morning to pick up your bright, yellow, free-lunch card. *Easy credit ripoffs!* Shopping at Goodwill was only humiliating if someone saw you going in or coming out. *Scratching and surviving.* My mother refused to sign up for actual welfare (Aid to Families with Dependent Children) and took the food stamps only reluctantly, but still her humiliation at struggling was palpable, and infectious. *Hanging in and jiving!* In the documentary *The Pieces I Am*, Toni Morrison, who grew up in Lorrain, Ohio, said casually, "We were poor when poverty was not shameful," and I sat in the theater thunderstruck. Such a possibility had never occurred to me.

Good times.

All of which is to say books were not so much an escape—there was no escape—as an expansion. They showed me other possibilities for living, even if all of those possibilities belonged to white people. My mother filled the bookshelves in the living room with books, including a dazzling collection of *Reader's Digest* Condensed Books. Dazzling, anyway, to me. I worked my way through the set, staying up all night in summers reading boiled-down versions of novels like *Hotel*.

It is tempting for me to say these books featured no Black people, but that's probably not true. Probably they were sprinkled with Black characters, dusted with two-dimensional stock figures trotted out to provide some color or make some point, directly or indirectly, about the white protagonist. As Morrison showed us, Black characters haunt the imagination of white American writers, from Poe to Hemingway and beyond. A few years ago, I began keeping a list of short stories by white writers in which Black characters pop up, stories which are routinely assigned in writing programs: "Rock Springs" by Richard Ford, "Silver Water," by Amy Bloom, others I cannot now recall. These characters serve as either as Magical Negro or Looming Threat. And once you start looking, they're everywhere.

I read constantly, which goes a long way to explaining the memory of myself as a quiet, bookish child who stood outside of popular circles, lonely and unloved. But this memory is only partially true. I was never really *unpopular*, was not ostracized or bullied or harassed. Being smart did not make my classmates dislike me; the myth of smart Black kids being ridiculed for acting white is greatly exaggerated. While I was sometimes teased for talking "like a white girl" and while I was, once, called an Oreo, these judgments had more to do with my lack of hipness than good grades. My junior high classmates voted me Most Intelligent and Most Likely to Succeed and wished me well when, out of nowhere, I was airlifted to boarding school in New Hampshire. My Black classmates at Snowden Junior High in Memphis supported me. It was the white kids at Phillips Exeter Academy who fucked me up.

But it is also true that I was, in some way I could neither define nor articulate but always keenly felt, an outsider. At school I had many nice classmates but very few real friends. Nobody ever came to my house (this was partly because my mother did not, as she said, "like people," which I now understand) and I rarely went to anyone else's. At church

I clapped my hands and sang the songs, doing my best to mimic the goings-on so as to avoid bringing a spotlight on myself, but I never felt a part of what was happening, never did much more than mumble along to whatever was being sung or said. Every Sunday was like watching an intense, passionate performance in which I was surely being judged but which I could not quite believe. Likewise at home, where, as we grew into adolescence, my siblings and I took different tacks in dealing with the One Great Force in our life: our mother. I walked the line between rebellion and obedience, questioning not only my mother's right to control me but her capacity to do so. If she was so smart, what was this life we were living? If she knew so much, why were things so desperately hard? If she couldn't be bothered to listen to me when I was telling her the truth about myself, why in the world should I listen to her?

It must have been clear to my mother that I was different and that this difference was dangerous to a poor Black child, especially a girl. I've written before about her attempts to control me, to reel me in, actions and statements I saw as cruel at the time but which I now see rooted in both fear (for me) and, more painfully, a kind of unacknowledged anguish and, yes, resentment at the way her own possibilities had been snuffed out—by us. What happens to a dream deferred? My mother does.

Nobody ever asked me what I wanted to be when I grew up. I'm not sure that was a thing people asked Black kids back then. (Children were not really *asked* much of anything.) My mother made her expectations clear in ways both direct and indirect: don't get pregnant, get an education, don't be poor. How we achieved those goals was open but limited: she suggested the military.

When interviewers ask me when I knew I wanted to be a writer, I say, "Since I was very young, maybe five or six." But this can't be true, because the concept of a writer was as distant and unknown as Jupiter. All I really knew was that I loved stories, loved reading, loved books most of all. And I loved the library. When my mother still worked at the main post office she would sometimes take us to the big central library next door on Front Street. This was the same library (the structure had been renovated in 1958 but the location was the same) that Richard Wright wrote about in *Black Boy*. When Wright was a young man, the library did not allow Black people to check out books, so he borrowed the library card of a white coworker and forged a note to the librarian, asking her to give "this nigger boy" books by

H.L. Mencken. By the time we got to the library in the late nineteen sixties, Black college students from two nearby colleges had long since desegregated it through sit-ins. All I knew was that I loved the central library, an imposing, modernist building with an entry below street level and huge, vertical levers that looked like sails.

I loved too the North Side branch, one of two originally "Negro libraries." This branch was closer to home, just a mile up our street and down Vollentine Avenue toward the projects, near the "bad" high school our mother would not let us attend. I remember the glass-brick entry and concrete walls, the high widows and fluorescent lights, the rows and rows and rows of books. It was a cool and welcoming sanctuary, a place I felt immediately and completely at home. Libraries are one of mankind's finest achievements, one of the few, uncorrupted institutions in America. This is only, thankfully, because there is no money to be made.

It was in that building that one day I picked up a book with a pretty orange cover and a drawing of a flying, black bird. By junior high I had a pretty firm grasp on metaphor and so the title caught my eye: *I Know Why the Caged Bird Sings.* But it was the picture on the back that made my heart stop: a woman, looking down, her beautiful face pensive and thoughtful. A Black woman. A woman who looked like me.

Are writers born? Are writers made? I could say I walked outside, held Maya Angelou's beautiful face up to the piercing Memphis sky and vowed to become a writer or die trying. It would be fun to say as much, but it would be untrue.

Not everyone who writes is a writer. Not everyone born with the capacity to write actually gets to write. Some people come into the world already lonely, already wondering, already eager to pin down life and look at it closely, no matter what that examination may reveal. These people are writers and they will write or they will die. The death, as Alice Walker reminded us in her essay, "In Search of Our Mothers' Gardens," need not be physical. People die all the time without going to their graves. I might easily have been one of them. Discovering that Black women could be writers was a critical and necessary first step in my journey. But it was only a step.

•

I once sat on a panel with a Very Important Poet, a former US laureate. The event was a fundraiser; our job was to sit pretty before an audience and be interviewed by several high school students, aspiring writers all. After the usual round of questions—When did you know you wanted to be a writer? Where do you get your ideas?—one student, a young Black woman, asked us each to recommend a poet she should be sure to read. Or maybe she asked the Very Important Poet for some poets she should be sure to read. He went down his list; I don't remember who he said, only that they were all fine poets, and also white and male.

When he finished, I asked the young woman if I could add to that. She nodded.

"Audre Lorde," I began. "She's—"

The VIP cut me off, abruptly furious.

"Don't do that!"

A little stunned, I tried to regain my footing. "Do what?"

"That!" he sputtered. "What you're doing now!"

That, it turned out, was recommending a Black female poet to an aspiring Black female poet. Shame on me for suggesting Lorde, because of her intertwining identities, might speak to that young woman in a way the others would not. The VIP went on to babble about some kind of shared, American identity and also his pet poetry project in which he had recorded thousands of Americans reading their favorite poem and among these was an old Black man in Chicago (or wherever) who loved Longfellow and another old Black man in Detroit (or wherever) whose heart burned brightly for William Butler Yeats.

I am my mother's daughter, constitutionally incapable of backing down from a fight. The VIP and I went at it, hammer and tongs, audience squirming. After all, I had not suggested the young sister *not* read Yeats or Longfellow, only that she also consider a poet I was pretty certain she would not learn about in school (who was also an American, by the way, but never mind). Nor had I suggested that Lorde was only of use to poets who happened to be female and Black. Audre Lorde, Lucille Clifton, Frances Harper—these poets and others appear on every syllabus I create, though the vast majority of students who enter my classroom every fall and spring are white. But there is a difference in the reception, a critical one: what's bread to you is water to me.

When I teach Lorde (or David Walker or Harriet Jacobs or Zora Neal Hurston or Lorraine Hansberry or August Wilson or James Baldwin) to white students, they say, "Thank you for this, it's really interesting."

When I teach these works to Black students, some of them—not all, but many—say, "Thank you for this. It saved my life."

And I say: "Yes. I know exactly what you mean."

•

After college I began working as a journalist in Raleigh, North Carolina. A few years later I was in Philadelphia. By the time I was thirty I had reached the pinnacle, the holy grail, the *New York Times*. The first year was exciting; it was, after all, the *New York Times*. The building was right there *in Times Square,* for the love of Pete, and they gave you business cards with your name and that famous logo and people came to the phone when you called, even if it was only to lie. Plus, I was living in New York City, in Manhattan, in midtown, in an apartment owned by the newspaper; they wanted you close those first few months for proper indoctrination. I got a couple of A-1 stories and some pats on the back and, even though there was the usual low-level hostility from angry white men, I thought it would be okay.

By the second year the shine on my penny had apparently worn off. This seemed to be happening to many of the Black reporters, especially the women. Shuffled into dead-end beats, stories re-written with an iron fist, hung out to dry if something went wrong. From the outside, all the petty rivalries and back-biting and maneuverings of a newsroom (or a college department) look ridiculous; from the inside they feel like battle. At the same time, I was realizing I did not really like being a journalist. I had become a journalist because I wanted to be a reporter, failing to realize these things are not always the same. I had (and have) great respect for journalism, believed (and believe) that a free and fearless press is vital to a functioning democracy. That message came clear to me the first day of a journalism class in college, when the visiting professor, a grizzled newsman straight out of central casting, stood up and bellowed, "The role of the journalist is to comfort the afflicted and afflict the comfortable." That delighted me. It sounded like just the thing. Except, in practice, too often it was not.

The equivocations of journalism, the pretense of objectivity, the dangerous two-sides-to-every-story insistence were not for me. It felt wrong, though for a long time I assumed the discomfort was the result of my failings and not the practice of journalism. By my fourth year at the *Times* I could not take it anymore. Every story I wrote was gutted; not only did I hate the work, the work was killing my voice, or so it felt. My unhappiness seeped into my marriage, which only created more unhappiness, and the depression I had battled for years rose up like a tidal wave, threatening to sweep me away. In desperation, I forced myself back to writing fiction, which I had largely abandoned. For weeks I left the newsroom and went home to work on a short story. When it was finished, I asked a colleague to read it. God only knows why. He savaged it. Then he said, "I'm only being honest with you because you're tough and I know you can take it."

Talk about being wrong.

Lying on the floor of my apartment, crying hysterically while my husband was out playing darts, I knew I had come to a crossroads. Either I was going to find out once and for all if I was writer, which would involve quitting the *Times*, or I was going to remain a journalist and quite possibly kill myself.

"You are making the biggest mistake of your life," an editor told me.

"Possibly," I said.

I walked out of the old building on Forty-Third Street in January of 1996. For the first time since I was fourteen I was not earning money. For the first time since I was five I had no required place to be during the day. For the first few weeks I avoided leaving the house during the workday, not wanting people to see me walking around and assume I was some shiftless, welfare-cheating bum (ah, internalized racism). One day I had to run to the local drugstore for some feminine supplies. I remember walking in and being shocked at how busy it was. How were all these white people not working during the day?

My goal was to write a novel, though I had no real ideas in mind. I went to the library, checked out a few books on writing fiction, discovered the average novel is 50,000 words. With a goal of a thousand words a day I could have a first draft in fifty days, I told myself. Every morning as soon as my husband left for work I sat down at my computer and did not let myself rise until I'd written a thousand words. Two months later I had a draft. A month or so after that I had a second draft and then a third and then I sent the manuscript off to the friend of a friend who was a literary agent. He passed it on to another agent, a woman named Suzanne. She called me. I got dressed and went into the city to meet her. It was one of the best days of my life.

Two years after walking out of the newsroom, my first novel was published. It received wonderful reviews, including a blurb in the *New York Times*. Sales were disappointing; the publisher, having thrown my book against the wall to see if it stuck, threw up its hands. I didn't care. I had published a novel, was working on a second. That made me a novelist.

What it did not make me was a writer, though I didn't know that at the time.

.

A friend, reading this essay in draft: "You keep saying that Baldwin made you a writer but you never say how."

Indeed, it seems I have been circling this question for a long time, struggling to put into words why finding James Baldwin, reading his work, watching his interviews, connecting to his soul—why this changed me. There are other writers who mean the world to me: Lorraine Hansberry, Audre Lorde, and the queen, Toni Morrison. There are writers I like a great deal (Alice Walker) and writers I love (Graham Greene) and writers I loved for a time (Ernest Hemingway). Not all of these writers are Black women, which should please the VIP; some of them aren't Black at all. What they have in common, I think, is a willingness to look at things and see them as they are. This sounds simple. It is not.

Still, not one of these writers did for me what Baldwin did. But how to describe what that was; is there a word? Transformed? Transmogrified? Changed over? Washed new? Everything I write sounds either too mystical or too pedestrian. Baldwin himself would use the church as a reference, the language of salvation: *How marvelous the grace that caught my falling soul / He looked beyond my fault and saw my needs.* But I'm not Baldwin and I'm not certain I believe in salvation. I believe in survival.

Maybe if I make a list of all the vital lessons I learned from Baldwin, the answer will reveal itself:

- That clarity and courage are required, though they will win you no friends.
- That fear is the universal human condition; what matters is how one responds to fear.
- That innocence past the time when innocence should have departed is monstrous.
- That the artist has an obligation beyond herself.

But these lessons, as important as they are, are not the sum of it. Life is full of lessons; the trick is paying attention when the lesson arrives. Perhaps that's what Baldwin taught me, and what made me a writer: how to pay attention.

It seems trite when I write it down that way. Let me see what else I can say.

A few years into my career as a journalist, I was asked to sit on the board of the Duke University alumni magazine. At our first meeting we went around the grand, polished table telling a little about ourselves. One question we were supposed to answer was what we were currently reading. Every single man at the table ticked off a work of nonfiction: history, biography, business texts. When the spotlight turned to me, I (naively) expressed surprise that no one was reading a novel. At the time, fiction was pretty much all I read. After a long day's confrontation with the ugliness of humanity, the last thing I wanted when I got home was more of the same. Anyway, biography bored me (most of the subjects being what they were at the time) and history depressed me and it seemed that all one had to do to get the point of most popular general titles was read the introduction and a few good reviews. A novel, on the other hand, was an experience that demanded commitment, far more immersion than escape. A good novel might be analyzed or reviewed but it could not be fully explained. "A story is a way to say something that can't be said any other way," wrote Flannery O'Connor, "and it takes every word in the story to say what the meaning is."

When I made this point, the assembly laughed. "Oh, honey," said one of the few other women on the board, an older, sweet-scented southern belle. She patted my hand. "Men don't like stories. They only have time for what's real."

I was young then, more easily intimidated. I did not have sense enough to say, "Yes, and maybe that's the problem. So many men focused on the real instead of the true." I figured these men, successful and powerful and accomplished, knew better than I what was important in life. I stopped talking about the fact that I read fiction. But the reading did not stop.

All of which is to explain why, a few years later, when I began to investigate this writer named James Baldwin, I began not with the essays which made him one of the most important American voices of the twenty-first century but with his fiction. The truth is, I can't remember which novel I read first, but in the narrative I've constructed in my mind, it was *Another Country*. I went to the library and found it there. The only book on the shelf.

PART TWO

Women

somebody / anybody
sing a black girl's song
bring her out
to know herself
to know you
but sing her rhythms
carin / struggle / hard times
sing her song of life
she's been dead so long
closed in silence so long
she doesn't know the sound
of her own voice
her infinite beauty

—*For Colored Girls Who Have Considered Suicide*
When the Rainbow is Enuf, Ntozake Shange

FOR THE FIRST FEW YEARS of my life I took the company of Black women for granted, immersed as I was in a sea of them.

There was my mother, to start: a smart, thwarted, complicated woman, raising five children solo post-divorce, exhaustedly treading water as she tried not to drown. There was my grandmother, another complicated woman (complicated women run in the family), whose presence in our lives waxed and waned depending upon what else she was scheming. In her defense, she still had her own children to raise, the youngest being three years junior to my oldest sister. Aunt P was more like a cousin to me.

The other aunts were more like "regular" aunts. Aunt K was married and stylish, zipping around Memphis in a sports car, working at the post office, helping her husband in the store they owned, living what seemed to us an ideal life. Aunt J was sexy, smart and hip, utterly at ease with herself and her body, an accomplishment for any Black woman, then or now. Aunt S lived someplace far away but sometimes called on the telephone.

There was great Aunt Pearl: childless, hardworking, tough and wiry. In my memory she is always walking somewhere: to the corner store, uphill to her job behind the tall iron gages of the orphanage, down the street to our house to babysit us while my mother goes to work. There was great Aunt Annie: soft and round and powdery, so Holy Ghost holy she seemed to float in a cloud of light. Aunt Pearl would whip you while Aunt Annie would pray over you and I preferred the former. The whippings were short and afterward you might get an apricot fried pie.

Most important were my sisters. Two older, one younger (paired with a twin brother), me in the middle. The four of us girls were as different in personality and temperament as people can be and so we fought as hard as we played, but don't get it twisted: mess with one, mess with all.

At school I had many white classmates, but my real and closest friends were girls, usually Black. Last but not least there was church. The Church of God in Christ does not ordain women, but it would collapse without their organizing, fundraising, leading, strategizing, cooking, cleaning and general support. The preening rooster in the pulpit makes all the noise, but it's the hens who deliver the goods.

This was the ocean in which I swam, not noticing the water until high school, when it was suddenly drained (or, to be precise about the metaphor, I was fished out). Through a fluke of fate and the insistence of my mother, I was cannonballed from Memphis to New Hampshire, to an elite, white boarding school. The landing was not gentle. Suddenly I was one of a few instead of many, defined by my Blackness (and my southerness and my poverty) in a way I never had been at home. A few weeks after arriving, I was walking around the picturesque little town in which the school is located when a car drove past, a window rolled down and someone yelled, "Nigger!" at their top of their lungs. It was the first time I'd ever heard the word in that context, lobbed my way with the intention of doing harm. I ran back to the dorm and called my mother from the pay phone in the basement, sobbing hysterically. "Are they lynching you?" she asked calmly. "If they aren't putting their hands on you, you stay there and learn what the white folks learn."

I wouldn't have made it if not for the Black upperclasswomen: April, Melanie, Sandy, Andrea. They took me under their wings, showed me how to survive in that frozen white tundra by huddling together for protection and warmth. When you are a Black student at a white school, you have a choice: hang with the Black kids or hang with the white ones, align with Blackness or run from it. Whether or not this is fair is irrelevant; the middle ground is exposed and dangerous. If you are smart, you will choose a side. I chose Blackness, became a cheerleader (cheering was low-status at Exeter, only the Black girls cheered and there were no try-outs and still I did not last very long) joined the Afro-Exonian society, danced to the Commodores and the Sugar Hill Gang at the student center on Saturday night instead of dancing to Pink Floyd and the Knack at the gym.

My roommate was white and very pleasant and so were the other white girls in my dorm, mostly, but there was, and is, always a space between me and white women, a danger zone in which I risked being dinged whenever I entered. That space did not exist with the Black girls. With the Black girls I could cry about the racist Latin teacher who bullied me and lament how all the Black boys on campus went after white girls and laugh about what passed for fried chicken in the dining hall. With the Black girls I could let my hair down and not have to explain why I wasn't washing it every day. I did not have to be forever on guard against the casually racist comment, which is exhausting, or worry about whose tender feelings I would hurt when talking about that exhaustion, which is worse. I didn't have to explain why I dreaded the next day's class discussion of Faulkner or Melville, why I was weary of being the only Black face in the class. With the Black girls, I was just Kim. "I feel most colored," wrote Zora Neale Hurston, "when I am thrown against a sharp white background." It would have been harder to find a whiter background than early nineteen eighties boarding school.

Exeter was where I came to think of myself as a Black woman, first and foremost. It would be lying to say there was joy in this initially: my first year at Exeter was probably the closest I have ever come to hating myself. Suddenly I was fat and short haired and ugly, or so I thought. Worse, I had to slink back from classes every day and share a room with a girl who was everything I was not: white, blonde, athletic, popular. She wasn't even mean or arrogant or unkind, so I couldn't hate her or feel morally superior. Selfish witch.

What saved me from self-hatred was mostly luck. Junior year, the young, white wife of our young, white drama teacher decided to stage a production of *For Colored Girls Who Have Considered Suicide When the Rainbow is Enuf.* This was an astonishing choice. For one thing, the show was still relatively new, having premiered on Broadway only four years before. For another thing, the play requires a cast of seven Black actresses; there were barely seven Black girls at the school. I think the director, whose name was Suzy, pretty much went around recruiting us. The first time we gathered in that ugly, cavernous theater to read through the play, my heart bloomed:

> she's half-notes scattered
> without rhythm / no tune
> sing her sighs
> sing the song of her possibilities

> sing a righteous gospel
> let her be born
> let her be born
> & handled warmly.

For Colored Girls was the first confirmation that I deserved to be handled warmly. The rehearsals were a communion, a lesson for me in the value and necessity of sisterhood. Also, the production was a smash.

•

I graduated high school with a sense of myself as a Black woman I had not carried upon entering, and went to college hoping to find other Black women with whom to connect. But at Duke, sisterhood meant sorority: most of the Black girls I managed to befriend my first semester disappeared once pledging began. Black sororities have a long, proud history; they exist for a different reason than white sororities and I appreciate that. But any kind of groupthink makes me itchy, any kind of indoctrination, even a well-intentioned and willing one, makes me scratch my neck. I was no more likely to put on a blindfold and march around in designated colors emitting trademarked sounds than I was to join the Army and march around in fatigues—or to pledge a white sorority. In his essay, "The Artist's Struggle for Integrity," Baldwin wrote, "Art is here to prove, and to help one bear, the fact that all safety is an illusion. In this sense, all artists are divorced from and even necessarily opposed to any system whatever."

Instead, I tried out for a few plays and hung around with the theater crowd until I got sick of their nonsense. I then got a job in the costume shop and learned to sew. I started writing for the college newspaper, wrote book reviews and theater reviews and articles about the surrounding Durham community and articles about racism on campus. Oddly, it was the latter which got me in trouble. The circumstances are hazy now, but a group of Black upperclasswomen took exception to something I wrote—or perhaps edited or maybe was simply quoted in—and showed up en masse at my dorm one evening to interrogate me, or maybe to intimidate. They accused me, as I recall, of being a race traitor. The evidence was clear for all to see: I had not joined a sorority, I lived with a white girl (a friend from freshman year), and I had attended a wealthy, white prep school, which meant I was one of those rich, bougie, Our-Kind-of-People Black folks who looked down on the regular colored folks. This would have been laughable if it were not so devastating. The line had been drawn and this time I was on the wrong side. I defended myself fiercely but inside I was crushed.

After that, Duke was poisoned for me. I slunk through the rest of sophomore year as best I could, head down and heart scratched. The next year I went abroad. I chose the University of Edinburgh in Scotland, of all places, strictly because they spoke English and, despite a year of French, I was too cowardly to try Paris or Dakar or Abidjan. (What a mistake.) There were no Black women in Edinburgh, at least none among the American students I met in the dorms or the Scottish students I met in class. Some days I wandered the hilly, cobblestone streets of the city like a circus attraction, drawing catcalls and puzzled looks and open-mouthed stares as I passed—Edinburgh is far more multicultural now than it was then—a stranger in the village. Once, in a pub, a drunken Scotsman insisted that I was Diana Ross and begged me to sing. Now I would climb up on stage and disabuse him of his misperception but back then I was young and self-conscious and not a little afraid, surrounded by so much whiteness. I drank my shandy and left.

When I returned from Scotland I moved off-campus,

sharing a house with the one Black woman friend I had, a New Yorker and engineering student with whom I had little in common besides being tall, female and Black. The other roommate was a white surfer dude from Florida. I have no idea how and when he came along.

Meanwhile my family had scattered. One sister chased her dreams in Missouri, the other finished college in St. Louis and became a U.S. Army officer. My mother packed up the twins and drove from Memphis to California, following the sun and my grandmother, escaping the past and seeking a better life. There were no cell phones then, no texting or email, and long-distance phone calls cost a leg and an arm. In emergencies we found a way to help each other. Day to day, we were mostly on our own.

And so I found myself, for the first time in my life, largely sisterless.

•

When we have pleaded for understanding, our character has been distorted; when we have asked for simple caring, we have been handed empty inspirational appellations, then stuck in the farthest corner. When we have asked for love, we have been given children. In short ever our plainer gifts, our labors of fidelity and love, have been knocked down our throats.

—Alice Walker, *In Search of Our Mothers' Gardens*

•

James Baldwin had little interest in the inner lives of women. This is hardly a surprise. Men are interested in the bodies of women, in our presence as comfort or titillation or threat, in our emotional gifts of caretaking and affirmation and ego-buffering. They are interested in what women think of *them,* though usually not why we think it. They may even be interested in femininity, or at least its aesthetic, eager to either embrace it for themselves or vehemently deny. But of all the men, gay, straight or otherwise, which I have known through work and love and life, only a handful have been sincerely interested in my thinking. Men may ask, "What do women want?" but what they really mean is: "What's it gonna take for me to get from this woman the thing that I want?"

What is troubling about *Another Country* is not Baldwin's lack of interest in the inner lives of his female characters, but the suggestion that they have no inner lives—at least none that do not revolve around men. Somehow I missed this notion the first time around, sunk as I was in my own inner life. Like the novel, and its creator, I was swept up in the needs, wants, and desires of the men: Rufus, Eric, Vivaldo. They struggle with love and sex (often confused) and friendship and family and identity and, most vitally for Baldwin, art. Richard is lost because he betrays his art, Eric is saved because he does not (art requiring the same risk and vulnerability as love), and if Vivaldo is saved, his willingness to grapple with his novel as he grapples with Ida will be the reason why. Even Rufus (I would argue, though perhaps the book does not), is broken not so much because he falls in love with a white woman in a racist society but because he is fool enough to abandon his music for her. They meet at a club where he is onstage playing, her gazing up at him, him looking down. The next thing we know, they have moved in together in the East Village, and he has largely stopped playing gigs, unmooring himself.

Yes, the boys in the novel have a great deal to struggle with and think about. The women have only men. Cass admits as much during a conversation with Vivaldo. Cass's marriage is in trouble; she is wrestling with whether or not to address this issue by launching an affair. Vivaldo, taken aback not by her proposed solution but by her difficulty itself, says he always thought life was easier for women. Men, he says, have "to think about so many things. Women only have to think about men."

Cass laughs at this statement, but not because the statement itself is ridiculous. Because having nothing but men to think about is *really, really* hard. "Vivaldo. If men don't know what's happening, what they're doing, where they're going—what are women to do?"

Well. This is all well and fine for Cass. She has had her life handed to her on the stick of white womanhood. She moved from the care and protection of her father's house to the care and protection of her husband's, carrying with her always the impenetrable armor of her skin. She moves through the world both oblivious to, and assured of, her privileged and unassailable place. Even after she endangers her marriage by having an affair it does not occur to her that the fallout from her actions might involve losing custody of her children. When Ida points out this danger, Cass brushes it away.

"It could happen. But it won't."

Not until her husband learns of the affair and reacts with violence and threats does her insulation shatter. Not until she is faced, for the first time, with standing exposed before a cruel and merciless world does her innocence rip. "You begin to see that you yourself, innocent, upright you, have contributed and do contribute to the misery of the world."

Ida, on the other hand, has never been given the luxury of innocence. Black girls rarely are.

My own innocence was lost somewhere around the age of nine or ten, when the understanding that we were Black and poor and that these things were both shameful and connected began to dawn. For a long time, I assumed that poverty was universally shameful, that everyone who grew up struggling carried some residue of shame. Very early in life I realized that my mother was unhappy and that her unhappiness had to do with being poor and also, somehow, with us. Beyond this lay things I did not understand and could not explain and neither could anyone around me; if they could, they did not bother explaining them to me. Reading helped. Books offered escape while also showing me that everybody suffered (as James Baldwin said) and that sometimes people suffered over things I had never even considered. Which meant the world must be full of such things.

The church of my childhood also helped rid me of innocence; any illusion about my own unbroachable goodness was handily dismantled every time the pastor opened his mouth. People were born wicked, an unavoidably sinful affront to God; since I was a person and as yet unsaved I was as bad as anyone. This caused some psychic distress, of course. Were I in charge I might have framed things differently, might have cast sin not as the breaking of certain (arbitrary, conflicting, power-reinforcing) rules but the intentional or unintentional wounding of other beings, of the world and of myself. Still, in the end it was a useful lesson: by the time I was eleven or twelve I understood I was as capable as anybody of being rotten enough to make Jesus cry.

In the philosophy of Baldwin, the shedding of this kind of innocence is not a loss but a necessity. "People who shut their eyes to reality simply invite their own destruction, and anyone who insists on remaining in a state of innocence long after that innocence is dead turns himself into a monster," he wrote in the essay "Stranger in the Village."

Which is why Ida, the only clear-eyed character, should be the heroine of *Another Country*. She knows her brother is in mortal danger, while his white friends refuse to see what's happening. She knows that Rufus becomes obsessed with Lorna because of Lorna's whiteness, and that this obsession will only lead to trouble. She knows that love does not solve all problems. She even knows, and this is one of my favorites, that men are helpless when they are hurt because they "don't believe it's happening. You think that there must have been some mistake."

This is insightful stuff.

She knows white people like Richard have no idea who they are and this makes them both pitiful and dangerous. She knows that same whiteness has sheltered Cass and Vivaldo and the rest from the very simple truth that suffering is real, safety an illusion and innocence a fatal trap: "You don't have any experience in paying your dues and it's going to be rough on you, baby, when the deal goes down."

Baldwin puts blazing truth after blazing truth in Ida's mouth and yet all this wisdom fails to make her heroic. Like all the boys she has art (in her case, singing) but like Richard she prostitutes it, not out of greed but out of rage and fear. The result is that she verges on being what Trudier Harris in her excellent study *Black Women in the Fiction of James Baldwin*, calls "an elevated whore."

"You don't know, and there's no way for you to find out," she tells Cass,

> what it's like to be a black girl in this world, and the way white men, and black men too, baby, treat you.

> You've never decided that the whole world was just
> one big whore-house and so the only way for you
> to make it was to decide to be the biggest, coolest,
> hardest whore around, and make the world pay you
> back that way.

(This issue of whoredom, and its connection or lack
thereof to innocence, is a looming, thorny one in the novel.
But we will get to that later.)

What Ida knows about the world comes through clearly
in her dialogue. But what she wants remains, in some ways,
a mystery, because, alone among the major characters, we
never enter her point of view. There is a gaping hole at the
center of *Another Country* where Ida should be.

At first I thought this omission might be unintentional.
Creating one compelling, fully-rounded, three-dimensional
character in a novel is challenging enough; creating three
(Rufus, Eric, Vivaldo) requires the skills of a master. Perhaps
Baldwin simply ran out of steam. Or perhaps he was simply
less interested in the inner life of a Black woman than in the
lives of his other white and/or male characters.

But an unintentional short shrift of Ida seemed
unlikely from Baldwin, who was as firmly in control of

his work as it is possible for a novelist to be (which is to say, *not complete* control). After finishing what I thought was the final draft of this book, one evening I stumbled upon an essay in which Baldwin wrote about writing *Another Country*. In "Words of a Native Son," he calls Ida his heroine, and writes that he intentionally left out her voice because she had to be, for the white characters, the mystery that Black women are. The construction reminds me of Robert Hayden's great epic poem "Middle Passage," in which the reader hears the voices of slave traders, ship captains, white survivors of a slave ship rebellion and the poet-narrator, but never that of the poem's primary subject: the enslaved Africans. In this way Hayden not only allows the perpetrators to testify against themselves, but highlights the unheard, unacknowledged, unrecorded voices of the millions who endured the "journey through death / to life upon these shores." The poem becomes a kind of negative space.

Perhaps this is what Baldwin was after with Ida. She is the novel's lynchpin, the lingering connection between the dead Rufus and his living white friends, a reminder of their innocent complicity. Perhaps Baldwin means the love and struggles of the white characters to serve as the negative space that illuminates what it means to be a Black woman in America.

But what Baldwin thinks it means to be a Black woman in America is to be a mystery to white people: unknown, unknowable:

> In order to get this across, I had to put great lights around Ida and keep the reader at a certain distance from her. I had to let him see what Vivaldo thought, what Cass thought, what Eric thought, but what Ida thought had to remain for all of them the mystery it is in life, and had to be, therefore, a kind of mystery for the reader too, who had to be fascinated by her and wonder about her and care about her and try to figure out what was driving her to where she was so clearly going.

This is all probably true for white people—Black women are a simmering mystery, alternately fascinating and frightening—but it's certainly not true for me.

Nor is it true, as Baldwin seems to suggest, that the primary and perhaps sole source of Black women's (self-destructive) anger is the social destruction of their men. As it happens, the protagonist of my first novel *is* self-destructively raging against whiteness and white people, a thing I did not realize (see above about novelists not being in complete control) until I was interviewed by a radio talk show host on my first book tour. Prepping me beforehand, the interviewer asked what my novel was about. I said it was about a young Black journalist who was dating a radical Black activist and also a centrist white reporter and gets pregnant and on and on until she cut me off.

"Your novel is about how anger, even when it is righteous, is self-destructive," she said.

"Holy cow," I said. "You're right."

But my protagonist is not angry because society has deprived her of male protection by destroying her father or her brother. She's pissed because of what America has done to her mother and her sisters and what it will do to her if she doesn't watch out. That anger is huge and unfocused and dangerous, but it is exceedingly self-based. She knows she must put on her own oxygen mask first.

What Ida thinks, or would actually be thinking, is not really a mystery to me. When she finally breaks down and confesses to Vivaldo, she says she went down the long dark path she did because the death of her brother made her feel robbed, which resonates and feels right.

But Ida says the death of her brother made her feel robbed of the *only* hope she had. That part, for a Black woman, does not feel right.

·

> If Black women were free, it would mean that everyone else would have to be free since our freedom would necessitate the destruction of all systems of oppression.
>
> —The Cohambee River Collective Statement

·

For a handful of years after graduation I lived a largely white life. It was not intentional; more like a natural progression from the lives I had led in boarding school and college. I didn't try to make it happen, but neither did I try very hard to make it stop.

My first job was with the Associated Press in Raleigh, North Carolina, where I was the only Black person in the bureau. Next came a staff position at the *Greensboro*

News and Record in the city where the Woolworth counter sit-ins began. There were a few Black women on staff in Greensboro—one an editor in the styles section, another a librarian—but they were older, married, focused on other things. Haltingly, I sought out Black spaces in the city, uncertain where to look. I went to church, which was Black but not progressive. I volunteered for Big Brothers/Big Sisters, which was progressive (sort of) but not Black, at least not among the chummy volunteers. My limited social life revolved around my roommate (white) and my long-distance, on-again, off-again boyfriend (white) and my work friend and his lovely wife (Mexican-American). Unsurprisingly, I was alone much of the time. Unsurprisingly, I was lonely. Unsurprisingly, I thought the emptiness which dogged me cried out to be filled by a man.

Depression is biochemical, this much I know. Mine began in high school, intensified and relapsed throughout my twenties and thirties and forties until I gave in and took an antidepressant. Later, I weaned from the drugs but even now I remain vigilant. It would therefore be wrong to say it was disconnection from Black female support which caused the furious, teetering despair I so often felt during those years. But it sure as hell didn't help.

At twenty-five I landed a job with *The Philadelphia Inquirer* and was assigned to Bucks County, a wealthy, white county north of town. There were five of us in the bureau, plus stringers (freelancers who came and went) and everyone except me was white. It would have been easier to find Black folks had I lived in Philly and commuted to work in Langhorne but it was my first time in a big city and I was not quite ready. Instead I found an apartment fifteen minutes away in Bristol Borough, a place so quaint I thought I'd stumbled into *The Andy Griffith Show*. The apartment was right on Main Street, just blocks from the riverfront, across from a bakery, above a jewelry shop. I fell in love the minute I saw it but—and this only comes back to me now—I was also a little afraid. Before signing the lease I walked around town for an hour, holding my breath, waiting to see if the quaintness would crack and reveal something sinister. Surviving 400 years of white supremacy has developed in many of us a kind of racism Spidey Sense (driving through gorgeous northern California with my husband recently my Spidey Sense was tingling like hell). Walking around Bristol Borough, every person I passed was white. The Black population, when I looked it up, turned out to be six percent, which is low but better than it seemed that day. No one was unfriendly, but no one was friendly, either; after a decade back home in the South I found this studied silence difficult to read. I was just about to take a pass, figuring better safe than sorry, when I spotted an older Black woman coming out of the post office. My heart leapt at the sight of her. I scooted across the street toward her, grinning like a fool.

"Excuse me! I'm sorry to bother you but I'm thinking about living in this town. I just looked at an apartment. I was hoping I could ask you: is it all right?"

Without missing a beat, she looked me in the eye and said, "It's fine. You'll be fine." Then she went on.

Later I was transferred into the main newsroom. For the first time since high school I was back in the daily company of smart, thoughtful and funny-as-hell Black women: Vanessa, Marjorie. It was like rain in the desert; I bloomed. Four years later, when I left to join the staff at the *New York Times*, I tried hard to take those friendships with me, knowing I would still need to seek out day-to-day support in the snake pit. Fortunately, the *Times* was undergoing one of its periodic Colored-People-hiring-sprees (always followed by Colored-People-sidelining-and-undermining-until-they-quit-sprees). I found a good sister-friend (Charisse); we worked to keep one another sane. Outside of work, I joined a Black writing group, named after John Oliver Killens, led by a brilliant woman named Carol Dixon. Once a month I drove to Brooklyn and sat in a room full of Black women (and a few Black men) who not only understood where I was coming from but what I was trying to do, a change that both exhilarated and terrified. It's one thing to impress white people with one's writing: all one has to do is be just "tragically colored" enough without being too angry about it. But these artists weren't interested in that bullshit. Carol. Jude-Laure. Dianne. Beverly. Dahlma. They pushed me to drop the white gaze and see the world through the eyes with which I was born.

"Who are you writing for?" asked Carol. "Make sure you know."

I didn't, but I realized I had to figure it out. It is a dangerous thing for an artist not to know in which soil their roots are embedded, which sun they are straining to reach. Only a Black woman could have taught me that. Since that time it has been Black women—Callie, Valerie, Bridgit, and on and on—who have continued to teach me the most important lessons about living in the world:

> *Don't forget to dance.*
> *Keep your circle tight.*

Ask for the manager, politely.
Don't let these people get your blood pressure up.

Another Country posits that Ida struggles because the tragic suicide of her brother leaves her unprotected in a merciless world. Her father, who also might have protected her, is a drunken fool before the death of his son, a stunted wreck afterward. Vivaldo, the man she has chosen to share her life, cannot protect her because he does not want to see clearly what menaces it. Unless some man steps up, the book suggests, Ida is doomed.

But Ida's real problem is not the lack of male protection in her life but the lack of Black female connection. In "Words of a Native Son," Baldwin wrote that Ida, "operating in New York as she did, as Negro girls so, was an object of wonder and even some despair—and some distrust—to all the people around her, including people who were very fond of her —Vivaldo, her lover, and their friends."

With friends like these, Ida scarcely needs enemies. She is strangely, tragically, disconnected from Black women, trying to navigate the treacherous waters of America without sisters at her side.

No wonder she is lost.

PART THREE

Men

Every black man walking in this country pays a tremendous price for walking: for men are not women, and a man's balance depends on the weight he carries between his legs. All men, however they may face or fail to face it, however they may handle or be handled by it, know something about each other, which is simply that a man without balls is not a man; that the word *genesis* describes the male, involves the phallus, and refers to the seed which gives life.

—"Take Me to the Water"

HOWARD KEEL'S BEARDED, HANDSOME FACE. We are following him down the raised wooden sidewalks of a frontier town in the Oregon Territory as he appraises the women in a jaunty song that enraptures me and also makes me anxious in a way I cannot identify: *Pretty and trim, a little too slim. Heavenly eyes but* oh *that* size. Keel's character, Adam, has come to town from his backwoods claim to find the perfect bride. He has only the afternoon to accomplish this goal, but it takes only the length of the song. By the time he finishes he has found the woman he will marry and take home to meet his six brothers. The movie has begun.

I don't remember how old I was when I first saw *Seven Brides for Seven Brothers*. Older than five (when my parents divorced and we moved to Memphis), certainly, and younger than twelve, when the magic of technicolor Hollywood wore abruptly and permanently off. Let us guess seven: seven years of childhood when first I fell in love with Adam, Benjamin, Caleb, and the rest. Fell in love as I lay stretched out on the cold floor of our house with my sisters and baby brother, eyes locked on the television that was not only our primary source of entertainment but also our sole window on a larger, wider, whiter world. And, for me, the primary source of information about that strangest of strange things, the adult male.

It's not that there were no men in my family. My baby brother toddled around, playmate and victim. My Uncle Jesse was sporadically present, as was my aunt Catherine's husband. Later, in my teens, my Uncle Elmo, really my mother's uncle, would begin coming every Sunday to take us to his small, storefront church. From Uncle Elmo I would learn something about evangelical Christianity and something about patriarchy and maybe something about how black men, powerless and demeaned under a racist society, pass it on down.

But even Uncle Elmo operated on the margins of our real and daily lives, moving out in the shadows beyond the nucleus of my mother and siblings, beyond the realm of my grandmother and my cousins and aunts. Men were a dark mystery, another species of human being entirely, to be avoided and acquiesced to, desired and feared. My father, a thousand miles away and, as far as we knew, utterly uninterested in whether we died or lived, was both villain and unattainable standard ("Your father would have a fit if he saw a pan like that. Scrub it again").

What it meant to be a woman I knew; by the time I got my period it was perfectly clear. A woman had children and stayed with them, regardless of her own aspirations or dreams (if she even had any beyond having children). If she didn't have children, she took care of other people's, somebody's lost or struggling offspring always in need of being taken in. She took care of elders and neighbors and relatives; she worked collectively with her family to survive. She served humbly in the church, stayed out of the streets, and prayed. To be a woman meant caretaking, struggle, and sacrifice. But what it meant to be a man—what men wanted—was a mystery. And I needed to know, not because I wanted to be a man, but because I wanted to win one.

How to figure it out? One option might have been books; I was a child who lived to read. But the books I loved featured female protagonists: *Little Women*; *Little House on the Prairie* and the others; any Judy Blume or Judy Blume knockoff I could find. None of these books featured Black characters but the truth was, I didn't expect them to. It was enough, at least at first, to find a girl at the helm. In books I was searching for myself. To understand the mysteries of men I turned to Hollywood.

Thus *Seven Brides for Seven Brothers* and *How to Succeed in Business Without Really Trying* and *Holiday Inn*. Thus Tarzan movies (God help me) and Elvis movies (we lived in Memphis) and any movie with Rock Hudson or Cary Grant. These movies entered our lives through the television; we rarely went to the cinema. Thus also *Baretta* and *The Rockford Files* and my all-time favorite, *Starsky and Hutch*. What drove these men and moved them? What distinguished a good man from a bad man, a hero from a fool? What did these men want from a woman, other than that she be pretty and trim and have heavenly eyes? Or was that really all?

There were answers in those hours before the television, answers I absorbed without straining or filters, rain water straight down the well. Men were confident and selfless and unafraid. Men knew what they were doing; if they were doing a thing, that thing was probably right. Men became men by besting other men, usually through violence: in *Seven Brides for Seven Brothers,* Gideon, the smallest and youngest brother, displays manhood by standing up to Adam, punching him in the mouth. Men were sometimes nervous around women but it was only because they wanted the woman to like them. Men might not understand women but what came from that confusion was bemusement, never real and lasting anger. Never hate.

Most of this is untrue, as it turns out. This is not because the men who made these shows and movies were lying to me. The fantasies of masculinity that define American manhood are not deceptions but self-delusions, often desperate, sometimes sad, frequently destructive both to men and, yes, especially to women. To all our detriment, these men were lying to themselves.

•

Another Country is a man's book, a novel concerned first and foremost with the salvation of men. The fact that it contains two major female characters, one of whom serves as the fulcrum of the book, does not change this. The fate of the women depends upon the men in their lives. The fate of the men depends upon themselves, on their willingness to let go of innocence. The men of the novel are far more innocent than the women; they cling to this innocence far longer than the women and at far greater cost. They do so because they can and because letting go of innocence is frightening and they are afraid. Men, speaking generally, are far more frightened than women. This is a truth I did not understand at the time.

The most unfortunate of those men is Rufus Scott, a Black jazz drummer who commits suicide in the opening chapter. When I first read *Another Country,* it was Rufus who hooked me. For my money, Baldwin's taunt, succinct description of Rufus and his perilous state in that first, long paragraph is one of the best openings in American literature; if you don't feel something for Rufus by the end of it, you might as well go ahead and close the book. (Also check your heart.) By the time Rufus climbs the George Washington Bridge and leaps, I was heartbroken for his family, furious at

Leona and the rest of white America, and a little frightened for myself. The exhaustion of living as a Black person in a white supremacist society was not foreign to me, nor was the appeal of setting one's burden down. Plus, I lived less than an hour from the George Washington Bridge.

Rufus is brother to Ida, friend to Vivaldo and Eric, and lover of Leona, a white Southern belle whose arrival heralds his doom. The character was modeled on a friend of Baldwin's, a young poet named Eugene Worth, whose suicide helped drive Baldwin from America when he was twenty-two. On the surface, what dooms Rufus is a brutally dysfunctional relationship with Leona, a poor man's Blanche DuBois. In the hours before his suicide he wanders the streets of his city, broken and alone. He remembers not only his relationship with Leona but with Eric, a white, gay, actor whose love / sex has the power to heal almost everyone in the novel except Rufus. At one point he stands outside a jazz joint, faint with hunger and needing to use the restroom but afraid to go in for fear of being recognized and mocked, or, worse, pitied. A white couple leaves the bar, not seeing him; he is invisible to white America. They are killing him and they don't even know or want to know. Rufus keeps wandering. Leona has gone mad and been hauled back south by a brother, who tells Rufus that at home he would have him lynched. While his sister Ida desperately searches the city for him, Rufus turns to his friends, especially to Vivaldo, grasping for a lifeline. His friends try to toss him one but their toss is far too short.

Rufus kills himself because, as he says repeatedly, he has nothing left; "they" have taken it all: love, his music, his pride. Most of all, they have taken his manhood, because a man who cannot stand between the world and the woman he loves is not a man. In his essay "No Name in the Street," Baldwin tells a story of living in the Village and dating a white girl. Going out for an evening, they would leave the house separately, him trailing her to the subway where they stood apart on the platform and got on at opposite ends of the same car. They repeated the process at their destination and again on the way home. "She was far safer walking the street alone than walking with me—a brutal and humiliating fact which thoroughly destroyed any relationship this girl and I might have been able to achieve."

Baldwin translates this real-life experience into what Rufus encounters when he and Leona go out into the world. It eats him up, especially because he knows his friend Vivaldo can never experience that kind of emasculation. "The lowest whore in Manhattan would be protected as long as she had Vivaldo on her arm. This was because Vivaldo was white."

I grew up in a household devoid of male protection. My mother, ever-alert to our vulnerability in a dangerous world, was determined to protect us. Recently she told me a story about how my Uncle Jesse, her brother, once gave her a gun for self-protection. Though she appreciated the gesture, she feared having a gun in a house with five small children. She solved the problem by placing the gun in the bottom compartment of the stove, where it was forgotten. She did not think of it again until long after we had moved. "Whoever got that stove afterward must have had a surprise."

My mother taught us girls that protection was an inside job. We were not children who got in fights—I think I only got in one, brief physical altercation my entire childhood, after an older girl harassed my baby brother—but I always knew what to do if someone hit me: hit back and hit back hard. The goal, my mother said, was not necessarily to win but to make sure the other person suffered as much as you. "You might hit me," she liked to say, "but you're gonna draw back a nub."

When I first read *Another Country* I was married

to a white man, had "given him" (always a bothersome expression) one child and would give him another, but I did not feel protected by that fact. If anything I felt exposed by the attention we drew. Because we were living in "liberal" Westchester County, New York, the attention was usually more curious than hostile, but it was noticeable and often naked and always felt like it could turn on a dime. My husband, God bless him, was a good man but he was not a fighter. I always knew that if things went south I would not be standing on the sidelines, screaming helplessly, just as I always knew that I would always work regardless of whatever else I was doing (like having babies), would always keep some money flowing in. In my family there were no artificial assignments of duty; whoever was around, and it was mostly women, did whatever it was that needed doing. When my marriage ended and my husband moved out and I was alone in the house with two small children, I got a dog and an alarm system and a baseball bat and switched bedrooms so that I slept closest to the top of the stairs. I grieved the loss of many things for my children, but protection was not one of them.

But for Baldwin, the duty to protect and provide are manly duties, not only obligatory but defining. He was, for all his insight, sexual transgressiveness, and opposition to systems of any kind, still a man enmeshed in patriarchy. If you don't believe this, check out some of his interviews, including my favorite on *The Dick Cavett Show* in which he dismantles a pompous white Yale professor but does so in unconsciously patriarchal terms. This is how deep these channels of manhood run. My own husband (the new, permanent one), as feminist as a man who would not actually use that term could be, did not hesitate when asked for his definition of what it means to be a man: "To protect and provide for my family," he said, adding that by provide he meant not just financially but in terms of offering a good example, for his daughters, of how to live in the world. By protect he meant the straightforward, dictionary definition: to keep from harm. One of my favorite stories involves one of his sisters, a woman in her forties, who told him after her divorce that she was starting to date again. He took her to lunch and soberly warned her to be careful. "These men are just going to want to sleep with you."

"God, I hope so," she said.

As Rufus wanders the streets on the night of his death, he remembers a low point with Leona, when, driven nearly mad by demons, he debases and beats her mercilessly, accusing her of sleeping with other Black men, calling her a whore. Vivaldo tries to get him to stop but Rufus cannot control himself, can't even understand why he is doing what he is doing—all he knows is that white America is trying to kill him; the weapon of choice is emasculation, and he is trying not to be killed. "Sometimes I listen to those boats on the river—I listen to those whistles—and I think wouldn't it be nice to get on a boat again and go someplace away from all these nowhere people, where a man could be treated like a man." On his way to the bridge he passes white people who have the world on a string and know it. They stare at him with either hostility, which is bad, or with pity, which is worse. "He felt their stares but he felt far away from them. *You took the best. So why not take the rest?*"

A Black man's experience of racism is different from that of a Black woman. I'm trying to think of an experience of racism in which I felt the person attacking me (which is what racism is, an attack, whether physical or not) was attacking my womanhood, was coming after, to phrase it in the vernacular, my womb as well as my heart. I can't think of any. Every "microaggression" and moderate one (I have been fortunate) was leveled against the color of my skin, not the contents of my underwear. It took me a long time to understand this is different for Black men. They take it differently, whether it is meant that way or not.

But there is something else going on here, something the book suggests but does not really uncover. Rufus spirals downward because the racist society in which he lives prevents him from fulfilling his definition of manhood. But that was true before Leona. Before she walked into his life, the cops were still vicous, the landlords still slumlords, jobs still scarce. In a confrontation with cops or even white thugs, he would have been no more able to protect his mother or his sister than he was his white girlfriend. Yet Rufus is fine before Leona arrives. He has his music, his friends, his family, had "days and nights, days and nights when he had been inside with the crowd and the music and went home in peace and then woke, shaved and showered and went up to Harlem to his barber, then seeing his mother and his father, teasing his sister Ida and eating: spareribs or pork chops or chicken or greens or cornbread or yams or biscuits."

What Leona really drives to the surface is not just Rufus's emasculation by white supremacy but his internalized adoption of the same. Rufus, the novel makes clear, has made the fatal mistake of believing what white people say about him. His initial attraction to Leona is sourced in her white skin (and, especially, her southern white skin). The first time they have sex it verges on rape, Rufus turned on as much by the idea of violating a white woman as by Leona herself. Later he accuses her of being a whore not because of anything she has done but because only the lowest white woman would be sincerely interested in a Black man. He cannot, will not, put words to the inner demon driving him to the brink, but Leona can: Rufus thinks he's not good enough for her. On the bridge he looks out at the city in agony:

> He knew the pain would never stop. He could never go down in the city again. He dropped his head as though someone had struck him and looked down at the water. It was cold and the water would be cold.
>
> He was black and the water was black.

In his famous essay, "A Letter to My Nephew on the One Hundredth Anniversary of the Emancipation," Baldwin writes, "You can only be destroyed by believing that you really are what the white world calls a nigger." It is the combination of what Rufus has internalized about being a man and what he has internalized about being Black which forces him to the bridge. Like acid and bleach, toxic masculinity and white supremacy are dangerous enough alone. Mixed together, they take poor Rufus straight out.

•

For a few years now I have been trying to write an essay about trucks. I have the title—The Truckification of the American Male—but for some reason the essay refuses to congeal. Not because, perhaps, it's too difficult but because it is too obvious.

Still.

There was a time when the only people who drove pickup trucks were farmers or landscapers or maybe carpenters, people who needed the ability to haul large equipment and bundles of hay on a daily basis. I grew up in Memphis, which is the south but is also a city; my Uncle Jesse, who laid carpets and installed roofs, may have had one, but the car he drove to our house was a Cadillac.

But about fifteen years ago, when I divorced and recovered and re-entered the dating world, suddenly every man I met owned a pickup truck. One guy worked for a utility company, which perhaps made sense, but another guy was a lawyer and another a teacher and another an accountant and a bunch of them worked in tech, and they all drove trucks, either as their primary or secondary vehicle. This was in Boston, where the streets are tiny and crowded and meandering. Driving a truck in Boston is like riding a camel in Manhattan. You might think it looks cool but it makes no sense.

But trucks are now the best-selling (and second and third best-selling) vehicle in America, and not because they are cheap. The parking lot at my husband's place of employment is crammed every morning with these behemoths, their owners jockeying for the spots closest to the door so as to avoid having to walk any further than necessary from their rugged vehicles to their desks. Lunch hours are spent gazing at truck porn online, planning an upgrade or picking out amenities. Any man still driving a sedan is assumed to have "truck envy," and is either pitied or mocked.

Anyone who has watched a televised sporting event knows precisely what fantasy the truck makers are selling: a rough and tumble masculinity that needs no help and gets things done and rolls over anything that stands in its way. A masculinity unrestrained by rules or roads or boundaries, that answers to no one, not even a dying planet. The central tenet of American masculinity (and not just American but that's what I know best and what I'm talking about here) is the God-given right to do whatever I want whenever I want to do it, and to suffer no repercussions. To say this is infantile is an insult to infants.

The trucks are a kind of rolling representation of the masculine connection of sexual virility with manhood, with size, with dominance, and of the truth that manhood is established in the eyes not of women, but of other men (trucks are to men as purses are to women, says my husband). Going further, a truck is an obvious representation of its owner's sexual equipment, so obvious that the simulated balls some drivers string near the tailpipe just gild the dick.

That men are fixated on their penises is something no woman needs to be told. That they are nearly as fixated on the penises of other men as on their own is also not a surprise. In the novel, Vivaldo recalls a scene while in the Army and on leave with a Black buddy when they, drunk, whip out their dicks at a restaurant, ostensibly to show a nearby girl but really to show one another. What did surprise me was the realization that men think of their penises not as part of themselves *but as themselves*—the core of their being, the seat of their identity. Which explains why men think of women not as human beings with vaginas but as vaginas walking around encased in human beings.

This also helps to explain—sorry for my naiveté—why sex is so important to men. It's not just the pleasure; quiet as it's kept, sex is also pleasurable for women, at least if the other person knows what they are doing. (Which, if the other person is a man, is not a guarantee.) But in *Another Country*, almost every meaningful revelation, every moment of transcendence for the male characters, occurs during sex, as do most of the moments of debasement or humiliation. This is not true for the women. Cass is humiliated by her husband through word and violence while the one sex scene from her POV just kind of softcore fades to Eric sleeping on her breasts (ahem). Ida gets humiliated in public by Black male musicians and in private by Ellis, while we never get a sex scene through her eyes. But all the major male characters— Rufus, Vivaldo, Eric—get pages and pages of sex that is not just steamy but transformative. LeRoy liberates Eric. Eric gifts Rufus, heals Yves and Vivaldo, liberates Cass. Eric is a wonder, or his penis is.

In the novel it is during sex, when the penis is—for lack of a better word—*activated*, that the male characters are the most vulnerable and open, the most centered, the most, for lack of a better word, themselves. Whether this is true for the majority of men, I do not know, but it is interesting to think about. No doubt it is also true for some women, human sexuality being the great, expansive complexity that it is, but my guess is that it is less so, not because women cannot be unguarded during sex but because sex is not the only place we can be open.

And, disturbingly, the novel also seems to suggest that when men are most themselves, violence is involved. Nearly every love scene from a man's point of view in *Another Country* uses that very word, sometimes repeatedly; someone is always being beaten or tortured or driven, the penis wielded like a weapon. This is especially true if one of the partners is female (poor Leona) but also sometimes if the beloved is male, and it doesn't matter if the couple is dysfunctional (Rufus and Leona) or functional (Eric and Yves) or somewhere in-between (Vivaldo and Ida). "Love does not begin and end the way we think it does," Baldwin wrote in *Nobody Knows My Name*. "Love is a battle, love is a war; love is a growing up."

A growing up, yes. But a battle? A war? It is tempting to say this is a very male way of looking at things—an inability to look at things beyond a framework of conflict and aggression and dominance—and maybe it is, but men are not the only ones to subscribe to it. When I was newly married, a woman

I knew warned me to always make sure I had a "hand" in my relationship, by which she meant the upper one. In her view, marriage was a continuous contest to be waged; either I would win or my husband would, but a joint winning was impossible. This seemed to me an exhausting way to live. I would rather live alone than in constant battle. Fortunately, I know these are not the only options. Submitting to a relationship, to a third entity that is neither you nor the other person but the thing between you, the whole greater than the sum of its parts—this is not the same as submitting to the other person. Mediation is not submission. Negotiation is not dominance. Love is construction and restoration, a constant repatching and repair of the house. None of this requires aggression, except, possibly, against one's ego. But maybe this is a woman's way of looking at it.

In *Another Country,* love is a battle and since love is sex, sex is a battle too. Battle requires aggression. Aggression is male. Dominance is male. Submission is female. So is passivity. These are not the same things but they get all tangled up together in the novel. For man to be passive is to be submissive is to be feminine is to be despised. (There is a surprising amount of misogyny buried in this novel, but we will take this up elsewhere.) Rufus despises Eric's manhood by "treating him like a woman" in their sexual encounters, even though he was fond of Eric and grateful for Eric's love. Vivaldo, despite having sexual encounters with boys during his adolescence, associates gay sex with the humiliation and debasement of one man by another, in the same way he humiliates and debases the Black prostitute he sneaks up to Harlem to find.

And yet the novel also makes clear, both in several scenes and in so many words, that "the idea of being passive is very attractive to many men, maybe to most men." These words are stated by Eric. Vivaldo, listening, is skeptical. But later on, as they make love, he learns the truth of Eric's words:

> Now Vivaldo, who was accustomed himself to labor, to be the giver of the gift, and enter into his satisfaction by means of satisfaction of a woman, surrendered to the luxury, the flaming torpor of passivity, and whispered in Eric's ear a muffled, urgent plea.

Here is a truth about what it means to be a man that Hollywood failed to teach me: that the burden of masculinity is a great one, and that men, knowingly or unknowingly, sometimes yearn to put it down. What they don't want to put down, of course, is the power that accompanies the burden. But what the novel suggests is that letting go of the burden and the power can liberate. The opposite of aggression is not passivity but surrender. To surrender takes courage, but courage of a different kind than the one taught to men. Vivaldo, rising from bed with Eric, finds the courage to let go of innocence. He goes home to Ida, finally ready to stop pretending, finally ready to face the truth. His doing so is the only chance they have.

•

During college I got a job working as a hostess at a popular restaurant in Durham, a white hipster place where the young staff played REM on the stereo, consumed pot in the alley and coke in the john, and took turns sleeping with one another. I was out of my depth and way, way out of my comfort zone but a few staff members kept away the wolves and took me under their wing. One of these good people was Tom.

Tom was a white guy from somewhere in western North Carolina, with an accent so thick you could spread it on toast. He was older and calmer than much of the staff and seemed very mature to me, though he was probably no more than thirty-five. He had once been an evangelical Christian, but had left the church, and his marriage, when he realized he was gay. He was fighting to see his children but his ex-wife, who believed he had chosen the path of damnation, was fighting back. There was both a peace and a sadness when Tom told me these things, an acceptance of the complexity of life, of the fact that there are no guarantees. Tom still believed in God, believed in kindness and compassion and integrity. He was not perfect, just sick of self-delusion, trying hard to figure it out without harming anyone. Looking back, I think he was the first man I ever knew.

By this I mean not the first male human being. I had crushed on, been related to and taught, supervised, employed, harassed and coached by my fair share of such beings. It's possible some of those were men, though most of the ones I really knew were not. What I mean is that Tom was the first *adult male human being* with whom I sat and talked and listened and was listened to and really got to know. What I mean is that my definition of a man is simply that: an adult male human being. What I mean is that only a small percentage of adult male human beings ever achieve this status, regardless of how much money they make or how many relationships they have or what toys they purchase.

Now it is true that only a small portion of adult female human beings achieve that status either, but the portion is still much higher: say, fifty percent to ten. It is easier to be a man than a woman in the world but it is easier to *become* a woman than to become a man. The world, and especially America, is full of guys, some of whom are really, really sweet. But the world stands in dire shortage of men. Since Tom, it has been my great blessing to know a few. A fellow reporter named Juan and an editor named Gerald. The Reverends McLee and Williams. My friends Richard and Vincent and Daniel and Steve and Ron and Gary and Dave. My husband Ray.

That many of the men I have known happen to be gay is probably not a coincidence. Examining oneself, searching in the hidden, tender places for the myths and justifications and lies one has swallowed about oneself and the world, all of this is part of the hard but necessary work of attaining manhood (or womanhood for that matter, but we are talking here about men). It is far more likely, for obvious reasons, that a gay man will find it important to undertake this arduous work. In his essay "The Artist's Struggle for Integrity," Baldwin used that struggle as an analog for the integrity of being fully human, of letting go of selfishness and delusion and excuse: "It seems to me that the artist's struggle for his integrity must be considered as a kind of metaphor for the struggle, which is universal and daily, of all human beings on the face of this globe to get to become human beings."

In *Another Country*, the best man is Eric. He uses no one, abuses no one, lies to no one, especially himself. He sleeps with everyone (*everyone*) but these encounters are always respectful, always loving, always giving as much as he gets. Eric is true to his art (acting) and flourishes because of that devotion. He takes risks and grows from them, learns from his mistakes and does the same. He is not fearless but courageous, acting in full acknowledgement of fear. When he is sixteen and still at home in his small, Alabama town and in love with a beautiful Black boy named LeRoy, he is innocent, and that innocence threatens LeRoy's life. But when LeRoy tells him to shed that innocence or be the cause, as are so many white people, of casual violence and harm to others, Eric tries. The trying makes him a man.

Looking back over my life, counting up the men I have known, I arrive at a number that is not large but also is not small, not as small as I might have feared. There are men in the world, good men (which, one might argue, is a redundancy). This is reassuring because many women, deep down inside, believe no such creature exists. Women spend a fair amount of time wondering about men but the wondering usually takes the form of a question: *What the hell is wrong with men?* And the answers come quickly: Men are children. Men are selfish. Men are animals: dogs, pigs, goats, take your choice. Men are trash, say the women of a younger generation. For some reason, this one seems a step beyond. Children can grow, I suppose, and dogs have many redeeming qualities. Even pigs serve a purpose. But what do you do with trash but throw it out?

•

My husband and I are walking through a crowded parking lot. Ray is tall, fit, broad-shouldered. He walks with a stride that is just short of swagger, chin up, shoulders back, head on a swivel, scanning left and right as he smiles or nods or waves hello to everyone we pass. One day in the future, when we are talking about manhood, he will confess that he both does and does not want people to fear him, not in order to dominate, but in order not to have to fight. That is later, though; on this day we are maybe a year into our relationship, still learning the corners and contours. I know—and love—how he is but not necessarily why.

As we walk, a pickup truck turns the corner before us, driving way too fast for a parking lot. The driver is male, middle-aged, window down and music blaring, arm hanging out of the window as he surveys the land. He knows what he is doing, wants people to move out of his way and most do, including me. But my husband does not alter his trajectory. Sunglasses covering his eyes, he strides straight toward the oncoming truck. My heart leaps and I call his name, but just as I do, the truck slows, veers, continues on. At the entrance to the store my husband pauses, holding the door for me. I look at him, then step inside.

In her famous speech, later an essay, "The Master's Tools," Audre Lorde wrote that

> Women of today are still being called upon to stretch across the gap of male ignorance and to educate men as to our existence and our needs. This is an old and primary tool of all oppressors: to keep the oppressed occupied with the master's concerns. Now we hear that it is the task of women of Color to educate white women—in the face of tremendous resistance—as to our existence, our differences, our relative roles in

our joint survival. This is a diversion of energies and a tragic repetition of racist patriarchal thought.

When I was young, I thought it was my job to educate white people as to my humanity. Then I thought it was my job to alert them to the self-destruction of their own. I got over all of that. I never thought it was my job to educate men as to my existence and my needs and my humanity. The teachers of my childhood taught me men already knew these things. Even after I understood this to be untrue, I never felt obligated to educate men. Few men asked me to do so (unlike white women, who constantly demand my unpaid labor in their service). The men, I figured, did not really care.

What I know now is that my job, my only job, is to stretch across the gap of my own ignorance, to educate myself. This is my duty to myself as an artist and a human, and to my son and all the other men I love, and especially to my husband, who has tried his best to do the same.

Inside the store my husband shops in silence, waiting. In the checkout line I take his hand, smile. "I feel sorry for men," I say, only half-joking. "It must be hard."

He smiles in return, relieved. "No kidding," he says.

"Everything is an arena."

Everything is an arena. The insight of this statement stops me in my tracks. Everything is an arena, not just the boardroom or the basketball court but even the parking lot. Everything is an arena and you stand always in the center, sometimes in victory, sometimes in defeat. Everything is an arena and women are sometimes the audience, sometimes the enemy, sometimes the prize. Everything is an arena and you were born there and maybe you don't even realize there's a whole city beyond those towering walls and maybe you just don't know how to get out.

Though I teach creative and not academic writing, there is, nevertheless, a fair amount of instruction in the areas of grammar and rhetoric and style I must do for my students. For many years I approached this instruction through the lens of remediation: the students came to me deficient in the area of English language writing and it was my job to correct, or rather, fill, that deficiency. The assumption was that my students lacked fluency in real English and my job was to get them up to speed.

I do not see it this way anymore.

My students are already fluent in the many languages they speak. These are not only Spanish or Mandarin or

Portuguese, but also the language of South Side Chicago or small-town Texas or suburban New York, of second-generation or first-generation or military brat. They are not broken, nor is there anything deficient in them. They do not need remediation. What they need, simply, is help gaining a new fluency.

Manhood also has a language, one that intersects, for better or worse, with masculinity but is distinct from it. It occurs to me at this late hour of my life that it would be worth my while to gain this new fluency. Or at least to become conversant.

"Everything is an arena," I said, repeating after my husband. "Wow."

"Yes," he says. "I think I just realized that myself."

"That must be exhausting."

He says, "You have no idea."

PART FOUR

Sex and Sexuality

MANY YEARS AGO, I RECEIVED an email from an editor who was putting together an anthology of erotic stories by Black writers and who wanted to count me in. I was first astonished, then bewildered, then a little nervous. Just because I wrote fiction did not mean I could write *erotic* fiction. These are two similar but distinct efforts, involving the same raw material but producing different results. It's a little like asking a logger to whittle a hummingbird. Nevertheless, she persisted. So I sat down at my laptop with the window shades drawn. Eventually I delivered what must surely be the least-erotic erotic short story in history. It centers around what was apparently a real and pressing question at the time: was every white man who tried to get me in bed really just expressing "jungle fever" (I hate that term but as an appropriately despicable shorthand for the behavior I am referencing it will do). The story I produced was (is) so terrible I am surprised the editor accepted it. She must have been trying to fill out the book. Unfortunately, it seems to possess a half-life to rival uranium, popping up on Google searches of my name. When I was dating post-divorce I dreaded the day a man would confess, over a glass of wine, to having found a list of my books and ordered that one (usually only that one).

"I hope that doesn't embarrass you," the man would say, sort of hoping it would.

"I'm not embarrassed." I would smile, sadly. "But you're going to be disappointed."

Reader: he always, always was.

There is very little sex in my novels, as far as I remember. Maybe a scene or two in my first novel, less in the second and, if I had to guess, none in the third. To confirm these estimates, I would have to sit down and actually read my old work, but that is not happening. Nothing is more painful to a writer than revisiting the scene of a long-ago, never-to-be-repeated crime. Or maybe that's just me.

I'm guessing there's not much sex in my novels because I recall, more than the books themselves, the person I was when I was writing them: a harried young mother of young children, a recovering Pentecostal, a woman not much interested in sex. The characters in my fiction are concerned with identity and self-actualization (for lack of a better term) and, yes, also with love, love, love in all its forms and facets. Sex goes along with one particular kind of love, with Eros (the Greeks were so smart to differentiate the word; we fail ourselves by not following them) and so, in my novels, sex is acknowledged as an important part of the human erotic experience (I think). But any sex that takes place in my fiction is neither casual nor transformative. It's kinda just . . . sex. My goal in writing sex scenes was to get out as quickly as possible and avoid placing my work into contention for the Bad Sex in Fiction Award.

There is a fair amount of sex in *Another Country*. Every one of the major characters gets down with at least two people: Rufus with Eric and Leona, Vivaldo with Eric and Ida (and prostitutes), Ida with Vivaldo and Ellis, Cass with Eric and, presumably, Richard, and then Eric, in case it has not become apparent, with everyone. The sex is anything but casual, appearing sometimes as a battle, sometimes destruction, sometimes liberation. The sex scenes in *Another Country* are long, often running on for several pages. Far from pornographic, or even erotic, the scenes are more akin to descriptions of religious ecstasy, of wrestling with the Spirit, as is done in the Pentecostal church. (If we were discussing anyone but Baldwin here one might even say these scenes sometimes border on being overwrought.)

When I first read *Another Country* I skipped lightly over these pages, uninterested as either reader or apprentice. Like *Another Country*, the novel I was working on at the time, my second, was a love story. Like *Another Country*, it involved an interracial relationship. Like *Another Country*, it attempted to be honest about the ways in which, in a highly racialized society, race can get in the way of love, and also get out of it. That sex is involved in these issues is undeniable. But I was more interested in the meaning of that sex than the fact of it. The only thing *Another Country* had to teach me in this regard was that queer men placed as much emphasis on the act as did straight men. But I was a full-grown woman with many gay male friends by this point: that much I had already figured out.

No little girl grows up blind to the importance of sex to men. Setting aside the ways all of pop culture—television and movies and fashion and music and music videos— make crystal clear the importance of sexual attractiveness and virility and performance, little girls like me received the message directly in the form of a warning: *Sex is so obsessively important to men, to an extent we do not understand and for reasons we can't quite fathom, they will do anything to get it.*

Protect yourself.

By "anything" I here intentionally, if gingerly, include rape, because rape is part of what our mothers were warning us about. Generations of feminist scholars and activists have taught us that rape is about power, not sex, but our mothers did not make this distinction, possibly because they understood it was more complicated than that necessary-but-limited framework and decidedly because they considered the result to be much the same: the man who raped you and the boy who got you pregnant through seduction at sixteen both ruined your life.

But setting aside rape and sexual violence, setting aside underage sex and the problems which can arise, speaking strictly in terms of consensual sex within a committed relationship, the issue remains, for many women of my acquaintance, one of tolerant bemusement. Even if one has managed to rid oneself of the old canard that sex is something a woman endures in order to get the love she really wants, even if one actually enjoys sex, one might still not understand *why* it's such a *big* deal to men.

Perhaps this is where *Another County* can come in.

For the men in the novel (Baldwin, perhaps wisely, never attempts to convey a sexual encounter from the POV of one of his two female characters), sex is vitally important. It is also, in some ways, a paradox. On the one hand, it is almost always about dominance and submission. Rufus dominates Leona, even in their most tender (and first) sexual encounter. (After that things get really ugly.) Ida both fights against and submits to Vivaldo, who submits to Eric (in a separate encounter). Eric is dominated by Rufus, at first willingly and then not.

But what all this dominance and submission exposes is the tender vulnerability of everyone involved. Though the male characters are, as all Baldwin characters, unusually self-aware and self-expressive (if not self-fulfilled), they nevertheless remain, in daily life, constrained by the dictates of traditional masculinity: the necessity of being and appearing tough, of protecting girlfriends and wives and sisters, of not being bullied or bested by other men. The bedroom remains one of the few places they can allow themselves to be free from these dictates. During sex they cry and weep and relinquish.

If many women consider sex a painless, sometimes enjoyable necessary step in the acquirement of a basic human need, like grocery shopping, the novel suggests that for men sex is not merely a representation or outgrowth of love but love itself.

Here is Rufus, trying to tear himself away from New York City after Leona has broken under the strain of their violent relationship and been hospitalized:

> "I'm going to go. I just want to see Leona one more time." He stared at Vivaldo. "I just want to get laid— get blowed—loved—one more time."

Okay, so sex is not an expression of love, one among many, but love itself. Except—sometimes it's just curiosity and sometimes it's power and often it is violence and sometimes it's revenge, personal or racial. Rufus, having sex with Leona on a roof the night they meet:

> A moan and a curse tore through him while he beat her with all the strength he had and felt the venom shoot out of him, enough for a hundred black-white babies.

Sometimes sex is a sport and sometimes a battle and sometimes a game. Vivaldo, having sex with Ida:

> He had never been so patient, so determined or so

cruel before. Last night she had watched him; this morning he watched her; he was determined to bring her over the edge and into his possession, even, if at the moment she finally called his name, the heart within him burst.

Sometimes sex is affection and sometimes it's healing and sometimes it's liberation and sometimes it's some combination of the above. Rufus, remembering sex with Eric:

> But with his hands on Eric's shoulders, affection, power and curiosity all knotted together in him— with a hidden, unforeseen violence which frightened him a little . . .

I mean, I suppose if there were something that could be so many things to me, I'd be obsessed with it, too.

It is not easy for women—who risk violation, violence and death every time they step from the house, not to mention go on a date with or come home to or simply walk past a man—to feel sorry for men. It is not easy for women to acknowledge or accept the vulnerability of men, since that vulnerability manifests in a different, non-physical way. It is not easy for me to look at men—men who stride the world with the certainty that all they see was made for them—and feel empathy for all the confusion and fear and pain hidden beneath.

But it is important to do so.

•

I once got into a stupid Twitter debate (a redundancy) with a white woman who responded to some Baldwin quote I had posted by insisting that what drove the great man from America at age twenty-four was as much homophobia as racism. This homophobia, she politely informed me, was far more rampant among Black folks than white people. I responded that Baldwin had always been quite clear what he was fleeing when he fled to France as a young man: white supremacy. I linked to a famous clip of Baldwin on the *Dick Cavett Show*, elegantly dismantling a pompous white Yale professor who tells Baldwin he is overemphasizing racism:

When I left this country in 1948, I left this country for one reason, one reason only. I didn't care where I went, I might have gone to Hong Kong, I might have gone to Timbuktu. I ended up in Paris, on the streets of Paris, with forty dollars in my pocket on the theory that nothing worse could happen to me there than had already happened to me here.

But still the white woman insisted, as white women will, that her knowledge was superior to mine, that what she knew about Baldwin—and about homophobia in the Black community—was true.

"Everybody knows that much."

Well.

Another Country both is and is not a novel about sexuality. (Baldwin always said *Giovanni's Room* was not a novel about sexuality, either, but rather "what happens if you are so afraid that you finally cannot love anybody." The fear, in that case, being of facing who one wants to love.) *Another Country* is a novel about fear and love and innocence and masculinity and white supremacy and anti-blackness and also about the ways sexuality intersects with all of those things. But only secondarily.

The novel does not interrogate queerness. Eric remembers his coming-of-age as one of fear and confusion, but by the time the reader encounters him, that battle is long complete.

His challenge during the action of the novel has nothing to do with his sexuality. Eric, perhaps alone among the major characters, knows who he is. His challenge is to remain true to that person back home in America.

There is no homosexual self-loathing in the novel, which cannot be said of Black self-loathing. The reason for this is clear: Baldwin came to terms with himself as a queer man far earlier and more easily than he did as a Black man. This was possible because the black Harlem community in which he grew up did not condemn him for being "funny." Not in the violent, virulent way that "everybody knows" surely took place.

If there is little sex in my novels, there is even less examination of sexuality, for the simple reason that the topic did not much interest me as a young person. The privilege of being born into the majority is the privilege of not having to think about it, of concerning oneself with other things. I was straight, I knew I was straight, by the time it occurred to me I might, theoretically, be something else I was, as Vivaldo says of Eric, "condemned to men." Even the heartfelt pleading of a former boyfriend who insisted all women were bisexual (and therefore I really should be interested in a threesome with him) could not change my makeup. "Trust me," I told him, "If I could make myself interested in women, I would not waste time with men."

Like Baldwin, I grew up in the Black church. In Memphis "the church" almost certainly means the Church of God in Christ, the nation's largest Black Pentecostal denomination. The COGIC preaches that one must have a personal encounter with the Holy Spirit in order to be saved. It also asserts that the Bible is the literal word of God. This means (or at least meant when I was a child) that women should not wear pants or otherwise usurp the authority of men; believers should not drink or gamble or listen to secular music; and above all, sex is for marriage. It went without saying that marriage was between a woman and a man.

I mean that last statement literally: I do not remember hearing a single sermon against homosexuality in the church of my youth. Now, it's true I frequently endured the long hours at church by daydreaming, so it is possible I was off in an imaginary city living an imaginary life while the pastor raged against homosexuality. It's also possible I simply did not understand the language being used or the euphemisms being tossed. It's possible, but still, I find it interesting that I simply cannot remember any such talk. In the church of my childhood you were either saved, sanctified and filled with the Holy Spirit or you were not, and if you weren't you were sliding straight to hell and the shape of your particular slide didn't really matter.

If, on the other hand, you came to church every Sunday and cried and praised and shouted and caught the Holy Ghost, you were pretty much given a pass, as long as no one saw you drinking or sneaking around at clubs the rest of the week. Those were the sins I remember being warned against: alcohol, drugs, fornication (i.e. being a loose woman) and going to clubs (which is where all those things came into play). There was also failing to honor your father and mother and most damningly of all, hardening one's heart against God. *Curse God and die* was a thing adults said, meaning if you were stupid enough to do one, the other would surely come. (This is not precisely what Job's wife meant by those words but never mind.) Nor were we kids ever allowed to call one another fools; a fool was someone who did not believe in God. Your brother might be a dummy or a turkey but he was not a fool.

What did I know? What did I see? I search my memory for pop culture expressions of homosexuality. It comes back that a character on *Barney Miller* (a show we loved) was gay and so was a guy on *The Bob Newhart Show* and so was

Phyllis's brother on *The Mary Tyler Moore Show* (who didn't love Mary and all her wacky friends?) Elton John and Little Richard. Liberace and *Three's Company*. My mother never said we could not watch that silly, jiggly sitcom, never said that Jack's pretend homosexuality was corrupting our brains. Jack was handsome and funny and kind and Mr. Roper, the neighborhood's resident homophobe, was a laughable idiot. So was Archie Bunker, who mocked one of his son-in-law's friends for being effeminate then was shocked when his old, football-playing pal said he was gay. It was clear whose side we were supposed to take in these matters. Neither Mr. Roper nor Archie was who you wanted to be.

At boarding school, I was far too busy treading the choppy waters of race and class and gender to think about other people's sexuality. Looking back, I see how much more "woke" I was than my classmates about some things, and how much more asleep about others. The boy who played Jesus in our production of *Jesus Christ Superstar* was tall and blond and handsome and all the girls swooned over his golden locks and golden voice: it never occurred to me that he might be gay. On some level I understood that the drama teacher was gay and also the man he hired as an intern and also, perhaps, the teacher who lived in my dorm and coached field hockey—but who had bandwidth for contemplating the private lives of teachers? The first time it occurred to me that real people, i.e. people my age, might be interested in sex with people of the same gender was senior year. A group of us had escaped to the beach to celebrate the end of our Exeter experience. Giddy and exhilarated, a friend and I grabbed hands and ran across the sand, laughing. We were spinning like children when a boy on whom I had a crush appeared, smiling. "Are you two lesbians?" The question was not hostile, just curious (and probably excited) but I dropped my friend's hand like it was suddenly molten lead. "No!"

Forty years on, I consider my reaction with shame, and not only because it turned out my friend was, in fact, a lesbian (I don't know if she knew it at the time or not). Though I think my reaction stemmed more from disappointment that a boy I liked did not see me in the way I wanted than any feelings about lesbians, I wish I had reacted differently. Still, I can find no mention of the moment in my journal from the time, which means that was the end of it. My friend and I remained friends.

But *everybody knows* Black people are relentlessly homophobic, right? Everybody knows we are far more unyielding than white Americans in this regard. Everybody knows Black people won't support gay marriage or a gay presidential candidate or even their own gay children, so intense is this antagonism. Everybody knows the root of this long-standing antipathy rests firmly in the Black church.

Everybody knows all this so well and so deeply that for a while I doubted my own memories. Perhaps I had been daydreaming during those sermons, transported away. Perhaps, suggested my white husband, "Nobody bothered to condemn homosexuality because there were no homosexuals around. Or maybe people just stayed deep in the closet."

Except that anybody who has been to a Black church knows better than *that*.

In a 1984 interview with the *Village Voice* Baldwin said he never heard anti-gay rhetoric in the church of his childhood:

Not in the church I grew up in. I'm sure that's still true. Everyone is a child of God, according to us.

Didn't people ever call you faggot uptown?

Of course. But there's a difference in the way it's used. It's got less venom, at least in my experience. I don't know of anyone who has ever denied his brother or his sister because they were gay. No doubt it happens. It must happen. But in the generality, a black person has got quite a lot to get through the day without getting entangled in all the American fantasies.

In *Another County*, Ida doesn't like the fact that Eric slept with her brother, but she doesn't like the fact that Leona did either. Her fear is that white people only used her brother; it didn't matter if the user was female or male. LeRoy is trapped in rural southern poverty not because of his sexuality but because of his race; Eric, his white lover, escapes.

In that *Village Voice* interview, Baldwin said:

A black gay person who is a sexual conundrum to society is already, long before the question of sexuality comes into it, menaced and marked because he's black or she's black. The sexual question comes after the question of color; it's simply one more aspect of the danger in which all black people live.

Beliefs about homosexuality track along lines of education, income and party and church affiliation, all of which intermingle with race. It is true for example, that fewer Black Democrats than white favor nondiscrimination protections for LGBTQ people—68 percent versus 84 percent. But 68 percent is still *most* Black Democrats. And it is more than the percentage of white Republicans, Hispanic Republicans, or white, non-college educated independents who favor such nondiscrimination protections.

None of this is to argue that Black people cannot be anti-gay. Homophobia and transphobia are as virulent a force in Black America as they are in white America, with sometimes deadly results. The Human Rights Campaign documented the killings of at least twenty-seven transgender or gender non-comforming people in 2019. The majority of these were Black transgender women and their deaths, by and large, came at the hands of Black men. And the testament of millions of Black queer people as to the discrimination, mistreatment, violence and abuse they have faced at their hands of their Black brothers and sisters is sufficient evidence of a problem we must address.

Nor, Lord knows, is there any denying that a great many Black churches, and a great many Black Christians, are ragingly anti-gay. I've sat in their pews, walked out on their sermons. I've seen the damage they inflict in the tears of people who find their way, wounded, to the Black church to which I belong, a church which affirms all people as the children of God, full stop. My church is not unique. Unfortunately, neither is it the norm.

But Black Americans have not historically been *more* anti-gay than white Americans, not in Baldwin's time and not in mine. To insist we are and always have been is simply—suspiciously—untrue. The science fiction writer Samuel Delany wrote of visiting his mother in 1985 after a *Village Voice* interview in which he was identified as gay. A downstairs neighbor, Mrs. Jackson, enthused over the article. His mother simply beamed with pride. Later she took him to see a play about AIDS. Later still, giving a lecture at the New York Public Library in which he discussed being gay, Delany looked up to see Mrs. Jackson in the audience, along with his sister and a bunch of other older Black women. Afterward they crowded around and congratulated him on his talk. Delany's point is that he never spoke openly about being gay with his family, but they knew and accepted it:

Along with the burgeoning tragedy of AIDS, I was reading many articles by gay men about the problems they had getting their families to accept their gay lovers. My family, however, was always immediately and warmly accepting of any man I ever lived with. My problems began when we broke up; my folks seemed unable to accept that such a relationship was finished.

"Why don't you ever bring over X these days?"

"I told you, Mom. He moved out. We don't live together anymore."

"Oh, well where is he living? Maybe I'll call him up and invite him over for dinner next Sunday. He always used to enjoy my Sunday biscuits so much ..."

The poet Pat Parker expressed a similar kind of family acceptance in a 1975 letter to Audre Lorde. Parker describes a trip back to her hometown of Houston to inform her mother that she is a lesbian: "It took me three days to get up the nerve. And when I tell her all she says is, 'Well, as long as you're happy it's alright with me.' How anti-climatic."

For many years, ashamed of my people, I believed the narrative that Black people were more homophobic than the larger community. That narrative did not help me make sense of *Another Country* because it is not a narrative which functions in the world of the novel. It was not a narrative that functioned, or existed, in the life of James Baldwin himself.

From whence does this narrative come? It's possible that it is entirely a lie. It is also possible that something changed in the 1980s and 1990s, that Black church resistance to homosexuality not only grew but morphed into something that met or possibly (though I doubt it) exceeded the anti-gay hostility of white churches. If that is true (and I don't know if it is), it raises the obvious question: why? What changed?

I don't know the answer. All I know is to be wary of any answer couched in the wisdom of the masses. Because what *everybody knows* often turns out to be so much BS.

Part Five

Who's Whoring Who

Asking only workman's wages I come looking for a
    job, but I get no offers
Just a come-on from the whores on Seventh Avenue
I do declare, there were times when I was so lonesome
I took some comfort there

                —Paul Simon, "The Boxer"

THERE IS AN ODD, MINOR undercurrent in *Another Country* that runs dangerously close to misogyny.

That's a strange, disturbing statement to write. I almost did not write it, in fact, and when I did, I couldn't decide what to do with it. I thought I might attach this little section to the essay on women in the novel, and then I thought I would attach it to the part on sex and sexuality. But this strange undercurrent is not really about sex or sexuality, nor is it, I hope, really about women. In the end I sent it here, to a quiet, darkened corner, where it can sit and think about what it has done.

•

Here is a list of the potential consequences of sex that I worried about when I was younger, in the order in which they worried me:

- Pregnancy
- Disease
- Pregnancy
- Turning out to have been some white guy's jungle fever fantasy
- Pregnancy

Nowhere on the list was being sexually promiscuous, or being seen by others as such. This was not from want of effort on the part of the adults who oversaw my raising. In the church of my youth, having sex outside of marriage was one of the top two sins for a woman, higher than theft or murder (both sometimes justified). In some regards, a woman who "laid up" with a man was worse even than the women who plied their trade down on Beale Street. A woman who was paid for spreading her legs was a prostitute. A woman who did it for no price, not even the price of respectability, was just a ho.

My terror of pregnancy kept me mostly away from boys, along with a kind of insulating belief in my own unattractiveness. Then too, from high school on I was surrounded by white people, often theatrical white people (I mean that in every sense of the word), people who were artists and musicians and hippie hangers-on. These people hopped beds like Peter Cottontail hops the bunny trail. Compared to them, I was a nun.

So I never worried about being a "ho" and I certainly never worried about being a whore, since nobody in Memphis ever used that word except, perhaps, when discussing the whore of Babylon. (I was probably twenty before I realized these words were the same.) The women in my work never worry about this either. They may worry about having their vulnerability exploited by men, of having, as Alice Walker wrote, their yearning for fidelity and love "knocked down" their throats, but they do not respond to this threat by deciding to become a whore. (Some women do, I guess, though far fewer than men seem to think.) Caught between the second and third waves of feminism they tread the relatively calm waters of enjoying sex without shame, while also not making an identity out of it.

But Baldwin was a man of his pre-Women's Movement time. *Whore* was a word he believed in, a word that appears so often in the novel it starts to mean *something*. Standing in

Washington Square Park, Rufus imagines the eyes of white people flicking over Leona "as though she were a whore" because she is with him. By comparison, Rufus imagines, "the lowest whore in Manhattan would be protected as long as she had Vivaldo on her arm." (An entire thesis could be written on this paragraph alone. But not here.)

Later, Rufus thinks about Jane, Vivaldo's older white girlfriend. Of all the women in the novel, Jane comes in for the worst of it. She is referred to, variously, as a "cunt," a "filthy bitch," and a "monstrous slut," one who drinks in a bar filled with "shapeless, filthy women" and "pale, untidy, sullen men who worked on the docks." Note that the men, who work on the docks, are simply untidy, while the women are filthy. But as bad as Jane is, Rufus takes her presence in Vivaldo's life as a sign of his friend's devotion, believing that if Vivaldo were ever going to betray their friendship for a woman, it would be a "smoother chick, with the manners of a lady and the soul of a whore."

What in the world does this mean?

In Part Two, the reader meets Eric's love Yves, whose mother is guess what? *A puntain*. A cocktail waitress who survived the German occupation by using her body and her wits: "Later, she says that she do it for me, that we would not have eaten otherwise. But I do not believe that. I think she liked that. I think she was always a whore."

Of course, this judgment lies in the eyes of Yves, not of Eric, who is Baldwin's stand-in, while the harshest judgement of Jane comes from Rufus, who is lost and clearly doomed. Likewise the statement that "a woman who admires you will open her leg for you at once, she'll give you anything she's got," comes from Richard, the least admirable character in the book. One might argue that Baldwin is critiquing misogyny, rather than joining in. Neither Vivaldo nor Eric ever go quite so hard against women, reserving their judgement for people who sell out their art or sell out their friends.

Nor does the novel condemn Cass, who, despite being married, pursues and sleeps with Eric. Her choice to have sex is not based on the need to survive in a hostile world (like Ida and Yves' mother) but on some vague, ill-defined desire to rid herself of safety and protection and, therefore, innocence (one thinks there might have been other ways). Yet she is never called a whore, not even by her angry, hurt and universally despised husband. In a moment of violence (which also condemns him), he calls her a bitch, a slut, and a cunt. But not a whore. And in her final scene in the novel she speaks with a newfound wisdom that clearly mimics Baldwin himself. Standing in a museum, looking around at her fellow citizens and talking to Eric about the future of a nation that is as blind as she once was, she says, "This isn't a country at all, it's a collection of football players and Eagle Scouts. Cowards. We think we're happy. We're not. We're doomed."

All of this points to women being taken seriously in the novel. But how then to explain offhand descriptions of, say, the women on benches in Washington Square Park as old and "slatternly" while the men with them are merely "gray-haired, matchstick?" How to explain that even minor female characters like Vivaldo's neighbor Nancy and Vivaldo's sister, both mentioned in passing, tend to be either sexually promiscuous or sexual manipulators or both:

> His daughter was turning into the biggest cock teaser going. She finally got married. I hate to think what her husband must have to promise her each time she let him have a little bit.

How to explain even Cass's random use of the word— "*You evil-minded whore*"—when describing a snotty, gossipy woman who wonders, while watching Ida dance with the powerful agent, if the man's wife knows where he is.

And how to explain, most of all, Ida? Grief-stricken and enraged by her brother's suicide, left alone and unprotected (because her father has also been broken and her mother is a woman) Ida decides that the world is one big whorehouse and the only way for a Black girl to survive is to become "the biggest, coolest, hardest whore around, and make the world pay you back that way." She steps into an affair with a powerful white agent, trading her body for help launching a career as a singer. This does not sit well with the Black musicians with whom she works. On stage at Small's Paradise, one of them whispers in her ear

"You black white man's whore, don't you never let me catch you up on Seventh Avenue, you hear? I'll tear your little black pussy up." And the other musicians could hear him, and they were grinning. "I'm going to do it twice, once for every black man you castrate every time you walk, and once for your poor brother, because I loved that stud. And he going to thank me for it, too, you can bet on that, black girl."

What to make of this? Is the objection that she is having sex, that she is having sex for gain or that she is having sex for gain with a white man—or all of the above? In her 1861 slave narrative, Harriot Jacobs wrote, "There is something akin to freedom in having a lover who has no control over you, except that which he gains by kindness and attachment." But in the world of *Another Country* a woman exercising this freedom is not only disrespecting men but emasculating them. (To be fair, Mr. Flint, who "owned" Harriet and wanted her for himself, probably felt this way too.)

Somehow I missed all this the first time I read the novel. Failed to connect it with Richard's violent reaction when he finds out Cass is having an affair, in which he slams her head against a chair, then slaps her, unfurling the trifecta: *bitch, slut, cunt*. Failed to connect it to the violence and degradation Rufus rains down upon Leona, and with Vivaldo's prolific use of Black sex workers. Failed also to connect it to another Baldwin character with whom the reader is clearly supposed to sympathize: Frank in *If Beale Street Could Talk*, who tells his daughters if they were any kind of women they would be "peddling pussy" to get their brother out of jail.

The generous interpretation of *Another Country's* obsession with whoredom would be that this question is the essential question for every human, *regardless of gender*. Richard loses his wife's respect when he sells out his art by writing a commercial novel. Eric is the novel's hero in part because he refuses to sell out his art, is willing to "use everything life has given him, or taken from him, in his work" and to make that work his life. Vivaldo too refuses to compromise his artistic vision, even if it means being stuck in a rundown, Village walk-up.

One major piece of evidence in favor of this view is Yves. A *semi-tapette* when Eric finds him, Yves is rescued by love and realizes he does not have to be a whore just because his mother is one. For this realization Yves is rewarded even further; the novel ends with him arriving in New York, stepping off a boat into the arms of Eric and a bright, new world. Equally, Eric is only able to rescue Yves after purifying himself: "And he knew that the only way he could hope to bring this about was to cease violating himself: if he did not love himself, then Yves would never be able to love him either."

Still, as powerful as this is, it does not quite balance the scale. The ungenerous interpretation of *Another Country's* obsession with whoredom would be that Baldwin sees this as one of two possibilities for a woman: either be a saint or be a whore. Whether she trades her body for food (Yves' mother) or career advancement (Ida) or money (Vivaldo's prostitutes)—or simply engages in sex because she enjoys it—it's all the same. It is only under the wing of a man that a woman is really safe. In fact, only under the protective wing of a (male approved) man is she a woman worthy of the name.

I think I missed this dangerous undercurrent the first time I read *Another County* because I had not been trained to look for it. The instructors in my childhood courses of What Men Are and Can Be had skipped that lesson. It is interesting, if unsurprising, how little the television of my youth reflected the misogyny and contempt of women that undergirds our society. How absent was the generalized fear and loathing of women from the big and little screen.

Certainly, the *nervousness* around women of certain men, usually otherwise intelligent men with thick glasses and short pants and awkward social skills, is a well-honed staple of situation comedy. Jerry Lewis and Urkel, Barney Fife and the *Big Bang Theory*: nerds all demonstrate laughable anxiousness around the opposite sex. But these characters do not, beneath their clumsy nervousness, *dislike* women. Their yearning anxiety never mutates into rage. Every sideways glance and vulnerable smile assures us: these guys do not hate.

The men who hate women in the movies and television are deviant sociopaths, skulking around in basements, kidnapping blondes to make coats of their skin. There is violence aplenty against women in film and television, but the narrative stance toward the male perpetrators locates them clearly and definitively outside acceptable boundaries, inexplicably broken beings the show's hero (Representative Man) will quickly bring to heel. Unless I am mistaken (and, being a woman, I can admit the possibility) there is not, and has never been, a major movie or television show depicting the kind of casual, widespread, routine misogyny that erupts daily on the streets where women walk or in the message boxes of online dating or in the workplace or on social media. I remember Angie Dickinson (*Police Woman*) and Sharon Gleason and Tyne Daley (*Cagney and Lacey*) and even Rhoda and Mary and Phillis sometimes not being taken seriously because they were women, but I do not remember them being hated for it.

But there is, in *Another Country,* a casual contempt for women. Several of the characters express it—though not, it is important to note, the hero Eric—but none so baldly and vehemently as Yves:

I do not like *l'elegance des femmes*. Every time I see a woman wearing her fur coats and her jewels and her gowns, I want to tear all that off her and drag her someplace, to a *pissoir*, and make her smell the smell of many men, the *piss* of many men, and make her know that *that* is what she is for, she is no better than that, she does not fool me with all those shining rags, which, anyway, she only got by blackmailing some stupid man.

The generous interpretation of all this contempt is that Baldwin was simply holding up a mirror to masculinity, letting it reveal both its beauty and its ugliness. The generous interpretation would say that a man as brilliant as Baldwin, a man who, after all, had great, lifelong friendships with women—women as brilliant and talented and history-changing as Lorraine Hansberry, Maya Angelou and Toni Morrison—could not possibly hold, even subconsciously, the troubled, troubling view of women and womanhood that an ungenerous interpretation would suggest.

And there is evidence to support this relieving conclusion. In a late but powerful essay, "Freaks and the American Ideal of Manhood," Baldwin recounts how growing up in Harlem, where he was sometimes called a sissy but never really felt threatened or menaced, and where, at sixteen, he was taken up by an older Harlem racketeer who loved him and took him around showing off to his friends (who did not object) shattered "all of the American categories of male and female, straight or not, black or white ..." When he moved downtown to the Village, where his existence became "the punchline of a dirty joke," he was bewildered by the behavior he saw:

> It seemed to me that many of the people I met were making fun of women, and I didn't see why. *I* certainly needed all the friends I could get, male *or* female, and women had nothing to do with whatever my trouble might prove to be.

But a different, less generous interpretation of all those words and curses and eruptions against women in *Another Country* might point toward something else, something Baldwin did not intend. The ungenerous interpretation suggests that these words and phrases and eruptions are all sprouts atop a deep taproot of misogyny, one perhaps connected to a young fear of seeming and sounding too much like a woman which Baldwin mentions in the "Manhood" essay. Or to early relationships with white women in the

Village, relationships which paralyzed Baldwin with fear and sometimes unveiled twisted motives by the women, who

> ...intended to civilize you into becoming an append-
> age or who had found a black boy to sleep with
> because she wanted to humiliate her parents. Not an
> easy scene to play, in any case, since it can bring out
> the worst in both parties, and more than one white
> girl had already made me know that her color was
> more powerful than my dick.

Well. I have little interest, and even less right, to put James Baldwin on the analyst's couch. I can go no further in wondering about the connection between sex and violence that exists in *Another Country*. I have, in the end, no idea what beliefs about gender roles Baldwin may have internalized.

It's surprising when one realizes that a man who saw so much and so clearly nevertheless possessed blind spots. It's surprising when one realizes that misogyny, like racism or homophobia or, really, anything, can lie buried so deeply that even James Baldwin, a man unafraid of digging, was not quite able to completely root it out.

It's surprising but it shouldn't be: it just means the man

was human. And that the work of becoming more fully human is the continuing work of a lifetime. That it is never, for any of us, done.

Guess who taught me that?

Part Six

Interracial Love

"I'd like to prove to her—one day," he said; and paused. He looked out of the window. "I'd like to make her know that the world's not as black as she thinks it is."

"Or," she said dryly, after a moment, "as white."

THE FIRST BOY I EVER loved was Black. His name was Charles; he was seventeen to my thirteen, tall, handsome, a smile like a movie star. We met one summer while participating in one of those work programs the federal government used to fund for poor, Black children. This one paid a group of forty or so kids to put on a show in a park on the banks of the Mississippi, a park overseen by statues saluting the Confederacy. I was part of the writing group, Charles was one of the actors, who were, of course, the loyal royalty. I was flattered by his attention, disappointed that it remained platonic. In retrospect I see a young man heroically enforcing a boundary. At the time, I thought I wasn't pretty enough.

The first boy I ever loved who loved me back was white,

after a fashion. His name was Geoff, spelled the British way, which I had never known. We met five minutes after I stumbled off the bus that had brought me, glazed and lightly terrified, to an elite New Hampshire boarding school. He was a junior to my sophomore (or upper to my lower, which is how students are pretentiously classed at Exeter), tall and lanky and side-grinned and he walked with the swagger of New York. His mother was a radical leftist, his stepfather Black and they lived in Harlem when Harlem was Harlem and loved it there. When he dumped me, I took it as personally as a Black girl in a white school is likely to take it, and spent the next two years nursing crushes. None of which amounted to anything.

In college I fell hopelessly in love with an older Black football player named Brent. That went nowhere, as did a crush on a model-gorgeous Black guy with whom I worked at an off-campus, Moosewoodian restaurant. By the time I graduated from college I had kissed a handful of boys but none of them were Black. For whatever reason, the men who pursued me were white. One of them pursued until eventually, six years after graduation, I married him.

Some years later I was sitting around a table one day with a group of Black women, aspiring writers all. We were part of a Brooklyn-based workshop named for the great John Oliver Killens, founder of the Harlem Writers Guild. I don't remember if we were actually workshopping at that moment, if someone was writing a story about love between a Black person and a white person or if we were just talking; we spent, in that sister-circle, almost equal time in these two activities. It was one of the reasons I so loved the group.

So, my sisters, real talk: interracial relationships are a complicated subject for many of us. On the one hand, most of the Black women I know have neither the time nor the interest to police the desires of Black men. (And it is the desires of Black men we are really discussing here: Black men are twice as likely as Black women to marry someone who is not Black, a gap that outdistances even that between Asian women and men.) Free country, choice is choice, love is love.

On the other hand, most Black women I know understand that neither love nor choice occurs in a vacuum. While only fifteen percent of Black men overall marry non-Black women, that number rises to as high as thirty percent for Black men with a college degree. And, like Asian women, the vast majority of Black men who marry "outside of their race" choose someone white. It would take an act of willful self-delusion to divorce these statistics from the foundational and lingering impact of slavery on the nation's psyche, from the elevation of white female beauty and the cynical devaluation of Black womanhood. It would take an ignorance of the historical idolization of white women and the concurrent debasement of Black women going back to folks like Thomas Jefferson, who compared Black women to orangutans while busily raping an enslaved Black teenager.

It would take an ignorance of the roles white women and Black women play in the work of Black male writers such as Richard Wright and LeRoi Jones and Chester Himes. It would take never having read Eldridge Cleaver, who said: "Every time I embrace a Black woman I'm embracing slavery. Freedom is a white woman in my bed."

Students do not love it when I quote that line.

Even as recently as the fall of 2019, some professional football player (or maybe it was basketball, I don't remember) had caused a dust-up on Black Twitter by referring to Black women as "bulldogs." He was responding to criticism of his white wife, except the criticism came from a man and his defense went after Black women. He went on to declare that Martin Luther King Jr. died for his right to sleep beside a blonde.

To ignore all of this, to wonder not about any individual couple but about the larger story would take, in short, a complete and total lack of sociological imagination. Which leaves me and many of my sisters out.

So we, my writing group members and I, were discussing interracial relationships for some reason I do not recall and then this one woman, a woman I did not really know, said she was actually more disdainful of Black women who married white men than the other way around. I was at this point still new to the group, a little intimidated. They were all native New Yorkers and I could barely find my way to the Brooklyn church where we met. Also, it was the first time in my life I had belonged to an all-Black anything outside of church (which I had largely abandoned) and I was both eager and a little fearful, afraid I would be judged not sufficiently Black. The founder, a kind, brilliant and generous woman who had brought me into the fold, knew that my husband was white but I'm not sure if the other members did; the issue had never come up and I had not made a point of bringing it up. I never did, either in white spaces or Black ones, though the reasons were not the same.

When white people (at least liberal white people) learned that I was married to one of their tribe, it made them happy. This meant, they assumed, I would not be bothering them about silly things like racism. Since this was not true and since I had no great urge to alleviate white fear of confrontation, I kept my personal life to myself.

With Black people, it was different. Black people spend far less time talking about white people than white people think (and secretly hope) but when the subject did arise I kept quiet unless someone said something with which I disagreed, and that was rare. White people talking about Black people say things like, "Those lazy, shiftless niggers are all criminals." Black people talking about white people say things like, "My racist boss made me train that white boy and then gave him the promotion" or "That racist bitch in the grocery store threw my money at me like it was contaminated" or "Those evil motherfuckers would blow up the country if a cop put his knee on the throat of a dog but when he does it to a Black man they don't give a damn." If someone said "The white man is a devil," I could and would raise an objection. But if they said "White people in this country sure act like demons," I had no retort.

And yet it's true I sometimes worried what Black people would think of me when they found out I was married to a white man. Of the handful of times I have been directly confronted for loving a white man, all except one were by a Black man. There was that time at a reading in Chicago, and that time teaching inside a prison. There was that time in South Africa, when a fellow reporter (American) who I knew from the past leaned over the dinner table and demanded: "Why are you with that white guy, anyway?" To say I felt attacked would be accurate.

These confrontations and others left me, if not confused about who I was, definitely uncertain about where I stood. That I wanted to be a member of our pack I did not question. That I would still so be allowed was the question. Had I been so marked with whiteness that my smell would keep me out?

So when an elegant, Kente-wearing Black woman I did not really know looked around the room and said, with utter casualness, "Whenever I see a Black woman with a white guy, I think she must hate herself," I said nothing at first.

•

Of the three interracial couples in *Another Country*, two are doomed from start. One couple involves two men, one a Black man and a white woman, the final a Black woman and white man. These intersections of gender and sexuality put a finger on the scale of each couple's chances, but what ultimately determines the outcome, the novel suggests, is not so much the outside forces which menace interracial couples but forces within.

The youngest couple is Eric, sixteen, and LeRoy, seventeen. In the small-town Alabama where they live, their friendship arouses a dangerous suspicion, one to which Eric is at first oblivious and then dismissive. But LeRoy, being Black, cannot afford to live in such willful innocence. He knows they have to stop and who will pay the price if they don't. He knows that while Eric can and will escape the restrictions of small-town life, he himself is stuck there, imprisoned by racism and poverty and the need of his family. Yet it is LeRoy who works, in Eric, "a healing transformation," by giving name and shape to the desire that drives him, by making it real, and making clear that, to become a man, which is to say to become fully himself, Eric must accept his desire for other men. Must accept who he is.

LeRoy is a minor character in the novel, appearing only in Eric's memory during the night before he leaves France and returns home to America to face his future and himself. LeRoy is meant only to illuminate Eric's past, a past which gave him the courage, unlike every other white character in the novel, to let go of innocence. He treads dangerously close to being a Magical Negro, more concerned about Eric than for himself. "Poor boy," he says over and over as they snuggle, and only the first time is gently mocking. Later, after telling Eric they have to stop seeing one another because it is dangerous and hearing Eric respond that he will protect him, LeRoy laughs: "You better get out of this town. Declare, they going to lynch you before they get around to me."

This, of course, would never happen; *they* might well beat Eric for being "funny" but they would never lynch him, not only because he is white but because his father is rich. Still, LeRoy comes across as more centered than Rufus, the only other Black male character in the novel. LeRoy's sympathy for Eric is born not of internalized racism but of love. In his brief hour upon the stage, LeRoy expresses disgust with his situation but not with himself. He loves Eric because Eric is handsome, bright, stupidly courageous and big-hearted. Eric, in other words, is lovable.

Not so much Leona, the white woman with whom Rufus, who is Black, falls in love, or at least in obsession. She is not beautiful, not educated or intelligent (though not stupid), not sophisticated or accomplished or strong. She escapes one man (her abusive husband) and immediately attaches herself to another, without trying to live on her own. She claims to love Rufus but makes no effort to understand what his life is like as a Black man, dismissing the very real emotional toll it takes on him. Her best quality is loyalty, as well as a kind of protective innocence, which fails, utterly, to protect her in the end. Rufus, stepping down from the stage where he has just played drums, only stops to talk to her because she is white; his interest heightens when her accent reveals her southern roots. He remembers being in the south while in the Army, being kicked by a white officer and unable to fight back. Leona will be his revenge. Leona will prove his worthiness. But in a moment of clarity, Rufus imagines what his sister Ida would say about the relationship:

> She would say, "You'd never even have looked at that girl, Rufus, if she'd been black. But you'll pick up any white trash just because she's white. What's the matter—you ashamed of being black?"

This, then was the question, and I studied how Baldwin revealed the answer. Sitting in a Village restaurant with the white folks, Rufus feels "black, filthy, foolish." He considers

Jane, Vivaldo's pre-Ida girlfriend, to be a "monstrous slut" who therefore "kept Rufus and Vivaldo equally to one another." And when Leona, of all people, assures Rufus "ain't nothing wrong in being colored" he responds with either coldness or violence.

Studying the novel, I admired how Baldwin, in placing the question in Ida's mouth, also answered it for her, the only other Black character in the narrative. Ida's clear, unflinching pride in her Blackness creates a little breathing room in the novel. Rufus shuffles and rages around his white friends but Ida strides into the lives of Eric and Cass and Richard and, especially, Vivaldo, like she is offering them a gift. Unlike all the men in the novel, including her brother, Ida is unimpressed by Cass, the White Princess. She knows how to handle the powerful white agent who lusts after her, at least at first. When Vivaldo muses about taking her home to his racist white family because it "might do them some good," she rightly calls bullshit:

> "Don't you think there's any hope for them?" Vivaldo asks, hurt.

> "I don't give a damn if there's any hope for them or

not. But I know that I am not about to be bugged by more white jokers who still can't figure out whether I'm human or not."

What threatens to doom Ida and Vivaldo (in addition to Vivaldo's innocence) is not internalized racism on Ida's part but bitterness about what the white world had done to her brother, and what it wants to do to her. There are two roles for Black women in America, Ida says: caretaker or sexual object, Mammy or Jezebel. She will not be the former and if that leaves her no choice but to be the latter, at least she can make them pay. This calculation is dangerous but at least it is clear: the problem is whiteness, not Blackness. *You ashamed of being Black* is not a question for Ida. It is, however, a question for Baldwin himself.

I didn't see that when I originally read the novel. It did not occur to me that a man so knowledgeable about the true history of Black people in America, a man so aware of the grace and strength and resilience that has kept us alive could not wholeheartedly love being part of that tradition. It did not occur to me that a man who wrote, "Our crown has already been bought and paid for. All we have to do is wear it," could be uncertain about that crown. It didn't occur to me that a man who wrote, "Whiteness is a moral choice," could in any way shape or form want to make that choice. But, of course, being ashamed of one's Blackness and wanting to be white are two distinct and different things. So that was my mistake.

The signs of the former are everywhere, once you see them. In both his essays and his novels Baldwin is forever describing Black people by their skin tone, forever describing even people like Lorraine Hansberry, who, by comparison to, say, her good friend Nina Simone, was smack in the middle of the spectrum, as "dark," though darkness and lightness are both utterly relative. In the short story "Come Out the Wilderness," which may have served as a kind of template for *Another Country*, Baldwin imagines the thoughts of a Black girl named Ruth who is desperately in love with a white man who does not love her back:

> He kissed her. They both sighed. And slowly she surrendered, opening up before him like the dark continent, made mad and delirious and blind by the entry for a mortal as bright as the morning, as white as milk.

In *Another Country*, the connection between Blackness

and dirt or filth occurs more than once. These moments are hard to read, though they do help explain for me the one Baldwin position I could never understand: his defense of *The Confessions of Nat Turner* by his buddy William Styron, a novel which opens with our great revolutionary leader writing that "my black, shit-eating people were surely like flies, God's mindless outcasts."

What's the matter? You ashamed of being Black?

Reading *Another Country* in my thirties, I pushed this aspect away, more unwilling to ask the question of my hero than of myself. What I know now is that there is no shame in Baldwin having internalized white supremacy: every person born and raised in these United States has, more or less. How could one not, given the pervasiveness in popular culture and public art and the version of history taught in our schools? That is the definition of cultural hegemony, in which the imposed view becomes the accepted norm. Whenever I teach *The Autobiography of Malcolm X*, students are taken aback at Malcolm's admission that even his father, a proud Black man and disciple of Marcus Garvey, favored Malcolm over his siblings because Malcolm was so fair.

In a conversation with a young Nikki Giovanni, Baldwin said:

It's not the world that was my oppressor, because what the world does to you, if the world does it to you long enough and effectively enough, you begin to do to yourself. You become a collaborator, an accomplice of your own murderers, because you believe the same things they do. They think it's important to be white and you think it's important to be white; they think it's a shame to be black and you think it's a shame to be black. And you have no corroboration around you of any other sense of life.

The difference between Baldwin and people like, say, Clarence Thomas, is not having internalized white supremacy. The difference is that some people, like Thomas, swallowed the poison whole and asked for seconds. And some people, like Baldwin, spent their lives coughing the poison up, spitting it out.

Had Rufus done as much, he might not have climbed the George Washington Bridge. Instead he closes his eyes against the question. Pushes it away.

•

The first time I read *Another Country* I was working on my second novel. *Meeting of the Waters* is an interracial love story set during the Rodney King uprisings in Los Angeles, which I covered while still a journalist. It focuses on Porter Stockman, a white reporter for a Philadelphia newspaper who is saved from a dangerous situation of his own making while covering the uprisings by Lenora "Lee" Page, also a journalist. Lee saves Porter's bacon, then disappears before he can thank her. Miraculously (ah, fiction) she is later hired by the same paper for whom Porter works. They begin a tentative relationship.

By the time I was struggling with the novel, I had, under the influence of my writer's group, been immersing myself in the novels of Black women: Alice Walker, Gayl Jones, Gloria Naylor, Zora Neale Hurston, and, of course, the great Toni Morrison. I moved over to Baldwin after a random dude at a book signing accused me of hating Black men; in self-defense I dragged Baldwin's name from my subconsciousness though I had only really read "Sonny's Blues" in a short story class. Back home I decided I should dig into this person who had saved me, somewhat, from public disparagement. I went to the library, picked up *Another Country,* and brought it home. Somebody was clearly looking out for me.

Meeting of the Waters alternates POV between my Black, female protagonist and the white man with whom she falls in complicated love. I wanted to do something with the lingering anger I had from covering the riots and to refute the nonsensical belief that love was "colorblind," but I also wanted to see if I could write convincingly from the perspective of a white man, if I could successfully imagine what the world looked like through white male eyes. I thought doing so would make me not only a better novelist but a more legitimate one. The question of legitimacy is a question to be tackled on its face if one is a Black woman writer, but I did not know that at the time.

To my delight, I discovered that *Another County* was also written from the points of view of both its black and white—and male and female—characters (though not from Ida's). This seemed an incredible gift, a chance to check my work against that of a master, and, if needed, to course correct. When I got stuck I would turn to the novel for reference: how did men think of women, how did white guys talk among themselves, how did you insert a flashback into the middle of a scene? How do you write an argument that does not come across as tedious bickering? How do you create characters about whom the reader will care? In *Another*

Country, the central couple of the novel, the one that hangs most in doubt, is Ida and Vivaldo. Vivaldo, like Porter, the white character in my novel, is an innocent. He enters the relationship believing he can prove to Ida that he is innocent, in her brother's death and of being white. He wants to prove that color does not matter in the end. He wants to prove that all you need is love:

> "I know I failed him, but I loved him too and nobody there wanted to know that. I kept thinking, they're colored and I'm white but the same things have happened, really the same things, and how can I make them know that?"

> "But they didn't," says Cass, "happen to you because you were white. They just happened."

Ida is the more realistic person in the couple. I was just coming to understand that men are the real romantics, the true believers in transformative, effortless love and it was reassuring to see a male writer get this fact right. When Cass asks if the reason Ida believes she will never marry Vivaldo is because she doesn't love him, Ida scoffs: "Love doesn't have as much to do with it as everybody seems to think. I mean, you know, it doesn't change everything, like people say."

No doubt I saw myself in Ida, responded to her desperate struggle to be seen by the man who claims to love her. No doubt I feared coming across as hard as Ida does, as armored, even if such amour is necessary. No doubt I saw, in the volatile relationship of her and Vivaldo, echoes of my own marriage, already strained. Oddly though, I did not make the connection at the time. I was focused on the world of my novel, not myself. This, of course, is one of the reasons that writers write.

A love story can have one of only two possible conclusions: either the couple ends up together or they do not. As I labored on *Meeting of the Waters,* generating scenes and connecting transitions, growing fond of my characters and trying to be true to them, I struggled with the ending. I didn't know how to answer the Big Question. My inclination was no: having them end up together after all the twists and turns and very real issues that separated them seemed like a cop-out and a betrayal. I am not a romantic and I was not writing a romance. (I had no idea that interracial romances were a large and thriving segment of the romance novel genre and that my novel would get mistaken for one of these and that some readers would be pissed.)

The first ending I wrote was a break-up. Craft-wise, it worked but reading it left even me depressed, and my editor hated it. Someone once said that a novelist is always writing about either the way she thinks the world really is or the way she thinks the world should be, so which was it? A novel is saying something, whether the writer intends it to or not, so what was I saying about the possibility of such love in the world? I sure as hell wasn't going to say it was easy, or transformative or colorblind or any such baloney but did I want to say it was, in fact, impossible?

In his essay, "The Artist's Struggle for Integrity," Baldwin wrote:

Most people live in almost total darkness . . . people, millions of people whom you will never see, who don't know you, never will know you, people who may try to kill you in the morning, live in a darkness which—if you have that funny terrible thing which every artist can recognize and no artist can define— you are responsible to those people to lighten, and it does not matter what happens to you. You are being used in the way a crab is useful, the way sand certainly has some function. It is impersonal. This force which you didn't ask for, and this destiny which you must accept, is also your responsibility. And if you survive it, if you don't cheat, if you don't lie, it is not only, you know, your glory, your achievement, it is almost our only hope—because only an artist can tell, and only artists have told since we have heard of man, what it is like for anyone who gets to this planet to survive it. What it is like to die, or to have somebody die; what it is like to be glad.

Another Country ends with Eric waiting at the airport as Yves arrives from France "more high-hearted than he had ever been as a child, into that city which the people from heaven had made their home." But the novel really ends with a lie-clearing, illusion-crushing, innocence-ending fight between Vivaldo and Ida. This is a good thing, necessary if difficult. Afterward, Ida sleeps and Vivaldo sits down to write. The ending is not definitive: maybe they'll make it, maybe they won't.

Toni Morrison once said, "[Y]ou can have your little message at the end, your little moral but the ambiguity is deliberate because it doesn't end, it's an ongoing thing and the reader or the listener is in it and you have to THINK."

Handing readers a pat ending one way or the other is the real cop-out. Uncertainty is what makes the fictional true.

•

In 2006 I published an essay in the *New York Times,* in a column called "Modern Love." The essay wasn't even my idea, interestingly enough. My third novel had recently been published and someone at the publishing house had an in with the "Modern Love" editor; they suggested I write up something to help promote the book. Not being familiar with the column, and not having much luck in the love department (which were probably related), I was reluctant at first. What would I write about?

"Maybe something about race?" the publicist suggested. "Since that's what you write about."

My novel was, in fact, more about motherhood than race but never mind. It turned out I *did* have something bubbling away in the back of my subconscious. I was back in the dating world after a twenty-year marriage and a painful divorce (a redundancy; if your divorce was not painful I have just learned something about you) and realizing I was going to have to take a stand on certain things. No dating men who were only separated. No dating men who voted Republican. Most importantly, no dating white men who believed racism was a misty-colored thing of the past, like corsets and smallpox, who declared themselves "colorblind" and insisted I be the same, who stomped through the world willfully innocent of the havoc being wrought by them and for them. I had recently broken up with such a man; his name was Jerry. He was a good man but he did not believe me when I said white supremacy was killing me and the people I loved. He insisted that we had, in fact, already overcome, that society was more or less equal, that my protestations to the contrary were simply lingering anger and bitterness. From where he sat racism was a done deal and whenever I pointed out an instance or an example of its operation in my life he dismissed it. But he loved me, he said. He really, really did. Why couldn't I see that?

"What I don't understand," Ida says to Vivaldo at one point, "is how you can talk about love when you don't want to know what's happening ... How can you say you loved Rufus when there was so much about him that you didn't want to know? How can I believe you love me?"

My essay was published online on a Saturday morning, though it would not appear in print until the following day. By Saturday evening the emails were already trickling in: a few supportive ones from Black women (none from Black men) and many, many more from outraged white people. What did race have to do with love? Wasn't love colorblind? Wasn't I the real racist? Wasn't it really people like me who were the true cause of the "racial divide?" Poor, poor Jerry! One particularly passionate and angry series of emails came from a guy who turned out to be a son of a famous writer, and, who, in a rush to judgement, actually misread the whole thing. (He later apologized.) By the next day things were so bad I asked a friend to perform triage on my inbox, weeding out the worst ones so I would not have to read them.

If I was taken aback by the volume of emails (who knew the column was so popular) I was not surprised by the tone. By this time I'd been around enough to know that rare was the white person who welcomed a report from the frontlines of the battle against white supremacy. I'd been called bitter by the best of them: classmates at Duke and Exeter; neighbors and fellow Christians (before I got wise and quit attending white churches); colleagues in the newsroom of the *Philadelphia Inquirer* and the *New York Times*. My own ex-husband, a kind and decent man, had been unable, for twenty years, to hear what I was trying to say about the ways in which white supremacy and its requisite violence was still very much alive and well and wounding me and my family and friends. As the marriage was crumbling and we tried to hold it together for the sake of the children, we sought out a counselor. When the counselor probed as to the source of the problem my husband said, "She hates me because I'm white." I was at first too shocked to be angry, and then suddenly too angry to be shocked. Later I would come to understand his family, good liberals all, backed him up in this assessment, to the extent that they relayed their judgement to my children (for which I struggle to forgive them). I was the problem. I was obsessed with race for no good reason. I hated white people.

If I were writing the essay today I would, I admit, do some things differently. Space limitations meant I had to reduce dozens of revealing moments down to one, which made my decision seem frivolous; it would have helped to have more context. And I might have said bluntly what I thought was pretty clear but obviously was not: the problem wasn't Jerry's white skin, the problem was Jerry's whiteness. "Whiteness," wrote Baldwin, "is a moral choice."

Still, I doubt such changes would have made much

difference. The outraged emails would still have flowed. I would still have been accused of hating white people. I can't think of a single Black writer or artist or intellectual who dared to question white supremacy in America who was not, at one point, accused of hating white people. As though hating white people would not be a perfectly reasonable thing to do. Would, in fact, be very sane.

"Do you hate white people, Ida?" Cass asks after Ida spends a long cab ride through Manhattan trying to explain to the white woman the facts of a Black woman's life.

"What the hell has that got to do with anything? Hell, yes, sometimes I hate them, I could see them all dead. And sometimes I don't. I do have a couple of other things to occupy my mind."

Do you hate white people? It is, wrote Audre Lorde, an old and primary trick of the oppressor, keeping the oppressed occupied with the master's concerns.

Do you hate white people? Is a question of no relevance for Black people in America. The real question is this: Do you hate yourself?

•

If this were a novel there would be a climatic moment when that question was answered for the protagonist, a scene near the end when some action she takes reveals with perfect clarity that she, in fact, dearly loves her Blackness. Is both proud and grateful for everything it means and everything she is. Revels in the legacy. Gets a real kick out of it.

Perhaps that moment would come when her daughter is born, or later her son, or when they point to the posters of Martin and Malcolm and Harriet she hangs around the house and giggle, or when she curls into bed with them, reading a book called *Nina Bonita* about a white rabbit so enchanted by a little girl's luminous black skin he gorges on blackberries and coffee and dips himself in black paint trying to imitate her.

Perhaps it happens when she gets a chance to hear Toni Morrison and drives three hours and stands in line another two and then Morrison is so brilliantly, gracefully, effortlessly herself our protagonist bursts into tears in the audience, scanning the white faces around her for understanding and finding none until she catches the eye of a Black woman across the aisle, and the woman smiles.

Perhaps it happens as she is giving yet another speech about "The Racial Divide." She is asked to give many speeches, usually on Rent-A-Negro Day or during Rent-A-Negro Month, and she gives these speeches to the blank white faces and they applaud politely and cut her a check and go back to business as usual and she begins to suspect that part of the problem is the speeches themselves and the language used: *tolerance, racial divide, diversity and inclusion.* The real words are *white violence* and *racial injustice* and *white supremacy* and she begins to use these words and the invitations to give speeches dry up, and she is happy. She realizes that she does not, as Baldwin says, care to be integrated into a burning house.

Perhaps it happens when she moves to Boston with her white husband, afraid of the city's racist reputation, which is not unearned. Searching for community she stumbles across a local television show called *Basic Black*, where smart, Black people discuss politics and culture and art and when the show is looking for a new host she gathers her courage and goes down to the station to try out, despite having zero television experience. She does not get the job but months later she is called back for a second chance and so she meets Valerie and Callie and Ron and Phillip and Peniel and many others and they become an extended family and every Friday night in the green room is like sitting around the table in someone's kitchen playing spades and listening to Al Green and being Black and she leaves every time replenished. The tank filled right up.

Perhaps it happens when she decides she wants her children to grow up in a Black church, wants them to know the rhythms and the songs and the language, to know all three verses of *Lift Every Voice* and how to answer "God is good, all the time." Wants them surrounded by aunties and uncles, by deacons and mothers, wants them loved and prayed for by a village, but a village that has freed itself from a lot of the stuff which drove her out of the church of her childhood. And then, after more than a year of searching, she finds what she is looking for when she walks through the doors of Union United Methodist and finds a church firmly rooted in Blackness, open to everyone and overflowing with love.

If this were a novel, it could be any of those moments or any of a dozen or a hundred or a thousand more or maybe, instead of saying nothing to the woman who casually suggested she hated herself, instead of letting the subject change and the conversation paper over the awkwardness, our protagonist would have slapped the table, thrown back her beautiful Black head and laughed.

•

"If I were Black I would have burned this shit down a long time ago," says Ray, my now-husband, the love of my life.

We met almost ten years to the day after the *New York Times* essay ran. I had finally, after many fits and starts, clawed my way out of what might generously be called a dysfunctional relationship and, after taking some time off from love, was contemplating not so much throwing in the towel as just folding it away. All those clichés that people love to trot out, all those tedious bromides and affirmations—*You have to love yourself, first and foremost; no other person can fix the holes inside; you have to be willing to be alone rather than be in something wrong*—had turned out to be true. I'd tiptoed back onto an online dating site but, after less than a week, had decided to stop. Not one of the men who'd emailed seemed more exciting than a Saturday night on the couch with a book and my dog. I went a few days without checking the site then logged back on to delete my profile. There was a message from Ray.

It was brief, grammatical, not overly familiar (*ooh, babe, hello dear, hey hot stuff!*) It did not pretend to know or understand the poem I'd posted in lieu of a profile, too lazy and ambivalent to bother selling myself. It simply said hello. Also, he was tall and handsome and had no pictures with trucks or guns or water skis or sports teams logos. I said hello in return. When I logged back onto the site a day later, his profile was gone. He had left a message: *I'm leaving this site. If you would like to continue the conversation, here's my email. Be well.*

In ten years of online dating I had gotten the various stages of triage down to a science. The first filter—reading profiles—took out eighty percent of men. The second filter —exchange of emails—took out another ten. The third filter —meeting for coffee—eliminated an additional five or six percent. The first date was a time to test attraction. The second date was a time for questions. If the man was white, one of them was this: have you ever dated a Black woman before? If the answer was "I only date Black women" the yellow flag went up. If the answer was "No, but I've always wanted to," the flag was red. "There's really no good answer to that question is there," one guy said and I gave him points for that, though it still did not work.

Ray and I met first for coffee. I sat in my car for ten minutes beforehand, unaware he had seen me drive in, wondering why I kept beating my head against the same, hard wall. He was waiting outside the coffee shop. We shook hands, then he turned me around and measured our heights. We'd had a running joke in our emails about women lying about their age, men lying about their height. He had not lied.

Inside the coffee shop we sat down at the only open table; as soon as we did I realized the woman at the next table was someone I knew slightly from work. After ten excruciating minutes I suggested we go outside, where the talking was a little easier, though the July sun was merciless. It was far from the worst first meeting I'd had, but it was also far from love at first sight. This, I would realize later, was fortunate.

On our first real date I walked into the restaurant and saw Mr. Dysfunction at the bar. This put a damper on things and I was distracted throughout the meal thinking again about the suffering that seemed to go along with relationships. At some point I asked Ray if he had Googled me. There were, I had learned, two kinds of men in the world: men who Googled you the minute they learned your last name and men who did not. One guy met me for coffee, got my last name and then spent the rest of the evening texting me his increasingly hysterical thoughts about all my work he found on the internet, especially the *Times* essay.

What does this mean for us? he asked.

Not a thing, I said.

Ray had not Googled me. He wanted to learn about me the old-fashioned way. I told him a little about my background. He told me about his: central Mass native, Good Catholic kid, French-Canadian, a family that was working-class poor, in some ways poorer than my own: his parents never owned a house. The divisions in his childhood neighborhood were more ethnic than racial: the French-Canadians versus the Italians, the Polish versus whoever else was left. He did not attend school with Black kids until he broke from his family's all-Catholic-school mandate and went to the local vocational high school.

At the end of the evening I said I appreciated that he had not Googled me. Then I said, to save us both time, "Maybe you should."

I was gone for a week, teaching a workshop on Cape Cod. Somewhere in there he emailed me: *I read the essay. I loved it. You are an amazing writer.* This was hopeful. When I returned we met for dinner in Harvard Square. Over seafood I asked the question: ever dated a Black woman?

"No."

"Have you thought about what it would mean to do so?"

"Yes," he said. "But I would like to hear it from you."

We talked for two hours, then walked through Harvard Square, holding hands. Normally I did not like it when men tried to take my hand; it felt weirdly possessive. This, however, just felt nice.

For our next date Ray suggested we go kayaking on the Charles. He learned that I am competitive and I learned that his ego is not threatened by a woman who can do things. After we returned to the dock I went into the bathroom in the boathouse. I finished my business in the stall, flushed the toilet, came out into the room. A white woman stood at the sink, washing her hands. She looked into the mirror, saw me, and let out a yelp. By the time she recovered, I had washed my hands and gone. Ray was waiting outside in the lobby. As we talked, planning what to do next, the white woman came up to me, smiling broadly and chatting at top speed about how much fun kayaking was, etc.

When we finally got away from her, Ray said, "Wow, you really know how to make friends."

"Do you want to know what that really was?"

"Yes."

We went to a nearby bar for dinner, and there I told him. The woman had not been startled because she didn't know someone was in the stall: I'd flushed the toilet. She had seen a Black face coming up behind her and been frightened. And then she'd been embarrassed by her own knee-jerk racism. It was funny, I said, because just the week before, when I was on the Cape, a similar thing had happened. Every morning I rose early to run on the nearby beach, a small, bayside one belonging to the town. One morning I was all alone until three white women appeared in the distance, walking my way. When they spotted me they stopped dead. After a few moments of conspiring, they bravely ventured forward. There were three of them, one of me, and the town was wealthy, exclusive, and white: *I* was the one in mortal danger. I just kept jogging along the waveline and when they passed, calling hello and waving madly, said not a blessed thing.

Some white men, hearing these stories, would have told me I misread the women's reaction, was being unfair. Other white men would have said, "Oh," and changed the subject. A rare "woke" few would have taken over the conversation with their knowledge about how all "insecurity-driven oppressions" (a real phrase I once heard) are the same or how the real problem in America is not race but class.

Ray said, "That must suck, having to deal with that. Thank you for telling me."

Then he told me how he had spent the week I was away: he had ordered all my books, read the first and was working on the second ("You are really an amazing writer.") This was astonishing enough, but then he added that he had also watched the famous 1965 debate between James Baldwin and William Buckley at the University of Cambridge. The debate is quintessential Baldwin: eloquent, yes, but more than that. Buckley is eloquent; eloquence in the service of evil is still eloquence. Baldwin is like jazz, complex yet easy to follow, deeply passionate, chillingly cool. His performance always reminds me of one of those old cartoons where the rapier-wielding hero slices the bad guy so fast he doesn't realize he's been touched until he takes a step and falls into a dozen pieces.

But I had not told Ray about the debate, had just apparently mentioned Baldwin offhand.

"I thought I should find out about him," Ray said. "He's clearly important to you. Now I understand why. I can't believe I never heard of him before. He's brilliant. He wiped the floor with Buckley."

For a moment I said nothing. Then I leaned across the bar and kissed Ray.

"You ain't seen nothing yet."

Works Cited

Baldwin, James. *The Cross of Redemption: Uncollected Writings*. Edited by Randall Kenan. New York: Pantheon Books, 2010.

Baldwin, James. *Collected Essays*. New York: The Library of America, 1998.

Delaney, Samuel R. *Shorter Views: Queer Thoughts and the Politics of the Paraliterary*. Connecticut: Wesleyan University Press, 1999.

Gardner., John *On Becoming a Novelist*. New York: Harper & Row, 1983.

Harris, Trudier. *Black Women in the Fiction of James Baldwin*. Knoxville, Tenesse: University of Tennessee Press, 1987.

Shange, Ntozake. *For Colored Girls Who Have Considered Suicide When the Rainbow is Enuf*. New York: Scribner Book Company, 1997.

Wood, Spencer D. "African American Landowners." in *Mississippi Encyclopedia*. Oxford, Mississipii: Center for the Study of Southern Culture, 2017.

Acknowledgements

I am tempted to write "Thanks to you all, you know who you are!" and leave it at that. Because once one journeys down the path of acknowledgements, one is almost certain to trip.

But I would be remiss not to thank the people most responsible for this book: Robert Lasner and Elizabeth Clementson. Writing a book about my favorite novel would not have occurred to me had they not suggested it; in the middle of the project, I sometimes wished they had not. Certain books come to us when we most need them, during a time in our lives when the truth they speak or the comfort or confirmation they offer is like soup to a starving man. Going back later, when you are no longer starving, when the cupboard seems full and the pantry overflowing, is always risky: maybe the soup was not as tasty or nutritious as you thought.

Fortunately, that was not the case here. *Another Country* turned out to be every bit as nutritious as I remembered. Sure, maybe the seasonings could stand to be adjusted. But I know better than to mess with a master's dish.

Time now to abandon the food metaphor.

I would also like to thank my two beautiful and brilliant

children, for helping to build the person who meets the novel now, and mostly for being themselves.

Thanks to the fine women of my writing group, who listened to early drafts and provided valuable feedback. Thanks to my family, for tolerating a writer in their midst. Thanks to dear friends for tolerance and endless, loving support — you know who you are.

Thanks to Emerson College, for real and meaningful material support in the form of a j-o-b. Thanks to my students for giving me hope for the future of a troubled nation. Thanks to Black women everywhere, for showing up and saving the world again and again and again, not simply or even primarily out of altruism, but from the sheer necessity of saving ourselves.

Remember folks: "If Black women were free, it would mean that everyone else would have to be free since our freedom would necessitate the destruction of all the systems of oppression." From The Combahee River Collective Statement.

Most of all, thanks to Ray. Here's to you. Here's to me. Here's to us.